T0323586

Cambridge Elements ≡

Elements in Sociolinguistics
edited by
Rajend Mesthrie
University of Cape Town
Valerie Fridland
University of Nevada, Reno

DIALECTOLOGY AND THE LINGUISTIC ATLAS PROJECT

Allison Burkette
University of Kentucky

CAMBRIDGE
UNIVERSITY PRESS

Shaftesbury Road, Cambridge CB2 8EA, United Kingdom

One Liberty Plaza, 20th Floor, New York, NY 10006, USA

477 Williamstown Road, Port Melbourne, VIC 3207, Australia

314–321, 3rd Floor, Plot 3, Splendor Forum, Jasola District Centre, New Delhi – 110025, India

103 Penang Road, #05–06/07, Visioncrest Commercial, Singapore 238467

Cambridge University Press is part of Cambridge University Press & Assessment, a department of the University of Cambridge.

We share the University's mission to contribute to society through the pursuit of education, learning and research at the highest international levels of excellence.

www.cambridge.org
Information on this title: www.cambridge.org/9781009539388

DOI: 10.1017/9781009378567

When citing this work, please include a reference to the DOI 10.1017/9781009378567

First published 2024

A catalogue record for this publication is available from the British Library

ISBN 978-1-009-53938-8 Hardback
ISBN 978-1-009-37858-1 Paperback
ISSN 2754-5539 (online)
ISSN 2754-5520 (print)

Additional resources for this publication at: www.cambridge.org/EISO-Burkette

Dialectology and the Linguistic Atlas Project

Elements in Sociolinguistics

DOI: 10.1017/9781009378567
First published online: December 2024

Allison Burkette
University of Kentucky

Author for correspondence: Allison Burkette, allison.burkette@uky.edu

Abstract: People from different places use different words for things, even everyday things such as carbonated beverages (e.g., soda, coke, pop) or bread roll-based sandwiches (e.g., hoagie, grinder, sub). Regional variation in vocabulary is one of the foci of dialectology, a subfield of linguistics that examines the geographic distribution of specific words, along with distributions of different pronunciations and grammatical constructions. This Element will provide readers with a basic understanding of traditional dialectological study and will demonstrate through examples (audio, text, maps) how Linguistic Atlas Project research has changed and expanded over time. Readers will be introduced to the key concepts of dialectology with a focus on the North American Linguistic Atlas Project (LAP) and its materials. The Element will also discuss today's LAP with reference to third-wave sociolinguistics, outlining the ways in which the LAP has changed over time to meet the needs and goals of contemporary sociolinguistic study.

Keywords: Linguistic Atlas Project, dialectology, linguistic geography, sociolinguistics, historical linguistic data

ISBNs: 9781009539388 (HB), 9781009378581 (PB), 9781009378567 (OC)
ISSNs: 2754-5539 (online), 2754-5520 (print)

Contents

1 Studying Language Variation and Change

A dialect is a variety of a language that is associated with a particular group of people. Dialectology, the systematic study of dialects, focuses primarily on the regional or geographic distribution of linguistic features: vocabulary, pronunciation, and grammatical constructions. From the outset, dialect geographers (a.k.a. linguistic cartographers) had as their goal the delineation of dialect boundaries, an exercise interwoven with the creation of maps of individual linguistic features. This is not to say that dialectologists have not been interested in the connections between linguistic variables and social categories, such as age, socioeconomic factors, ethnicity, gender, and education levels, because they have, and have considered these social factors since the beginning of dialectological inquiry.

Investigations of "who said what and where" are, in essence, investigations of language variation. Add a chronological element of "and when" to also cover language change. Language variation and language change are intertwined; a lot of variation in language is the direct result of language change (and, to some extent, language change is dependent on having options in the form of variation for speakers to choose from). Variation and change are complementary aspects of language use and dialectology can teach us about both.

2 Brief History of Dialect Geography

The formal study of linguistic cartography began in Europe, where it can be traced back to the late nineteenth century and Georg Wenker, a German librarian who mailed a forty-question survey to other librarians and to schoolmasters in an effort to collect examples of regional speech in Germany. Wenker's questionnaire asked its recipients to translate forty sentences into the local dialect.[1] Of the 50,000 surveys he sent out, 45,000 were returned,[2] which understandably was both a blessing and a curse because of the tremendous amount of information that was yielded. Wenker dutifully compiled and published a series of hand-drawn maps, culminating in the *Sprachatlas des Deutschen Reichs* ("Linguistic Atlas of the German Empire"), which was published over the course of three decades (1889–1923) and whose completion, unfortunately, Wenker did not live to see. The *Sprachatlas* maps were information dense, with different regions distinguished by color-coded[3] outlines and differences in terms denoted with symbology. Figure 1 contains a close-up of the map for variants of the diminutive ending for "apple tree" along with a close-up view

---

[1] These were everyday sentences, such as, "In the winter the dry leaves fly around in the air"; "The good old man broke through the ice with his horse and fell into the cold water"; and "He always eats eggs without salt and pepper."

[2] What an amazing rate of return; can you even imagine emailing fifty people with a ten-minute survey and getting forty-five people to respond?

[3] Twenty-two different colors, to be exact.

(a)

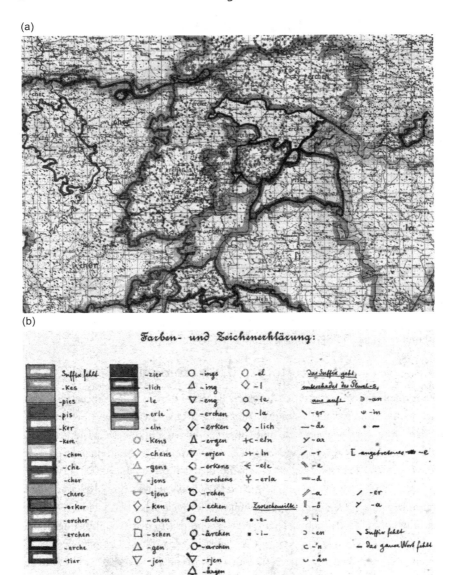

(b)

Figure 1 Two samples from Map 381 "apple tree" showing the different diminutive endings. Samples are from the *Sprachatlas des Deutschen Reichs* (Wenker 1889–1923), https://www.regionalsprache.de/SprachGis/RasterMap/WA/381.

of the map's legend. Clearly, the legend would have needed to be sizable in order to instruct map users on what the various colors and symbols mean.

The next iteration of language mapping included closer attention to pronunciation, as Swiss philologist Jules Gilliéron embarked on a dialect survey of

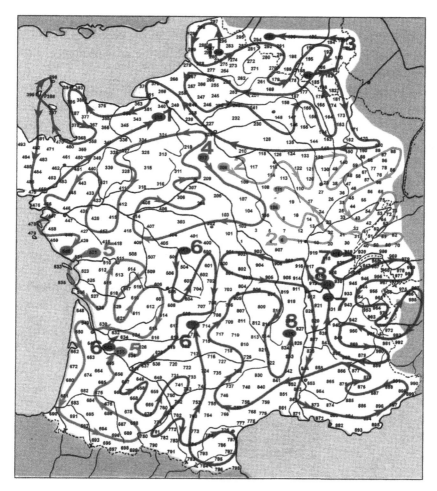

Figure 2 Edmond Edmont's bicycle journeys to collect data for the *Atlas Linguistique de la France*, 1897–1900.

France and hired a fieldworker to go out into the world and talk to people face-to-face. This fieldworker was a grocer named Edmond Edmont, who was hired by Gilliéron for his ability to transcribe – very quickly – speech into what was then the freshly minted International Phonetic Alphabet (IPA), a set of symbols that have a one-to-one correspondence with speech sounds.[4] Armed with the IPA, Edmont traveled across France on a bicycle (see Figure 2), setting in writing not

---

[4] Linguists needed something reliable. English spelling, for example, is a mess of letters that are only rarely faithful to a single sound and sounds that are not any more reliable in terms of how they're represented. IPA was invented as a reliable symbol-to-sound system that works for pronunciations in any language.

just the words that people gave in answer to his questions, but also how those words were pronounced. Between 1897 and 1901, Edmont interviewed about 700 people, collecting information that would result in the creation of the *Atlas Linguistique de la France* ("Linguistic Atlas of France").

Gilliéron had instructed Edmont to use a similar kind of translation-style question as Wenker had used, asking, for instance, "What do you call a hen-house?" But the next chapter in European dialectology moved from this type of direct questioning to an indirect method, one that would frame such a question instead as "What do you call the structure where you keep chickens?" Two of Gilliéron's students, Karl Jaberg and Jakob Jud, used this indirect method to collect information for their *Sprach- und Sachatlas Italiens und der Südschweiz*, ("Language and Thing Atlas of Italy and Switzerland"), published between 1928 and 1940. Jaberg and Jud were part of the *Wörter und Sachen* ("words and things") movement of the early twentieth century, which held that words and their meanings were inseparable and that understanding what a word means was essential to the understanding of culture. Thus, the resulting dialect maps often included drawings in the margins as explication, as seen in the Italian and Swiss *Sprachatlas* sample in Figure 3 showing a map of terms for "chest," accompanied by three drawings of different types of *cassettone*.

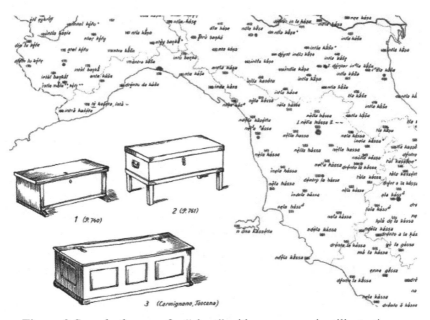

Figure 3 *Sprachatlas* map for "chest" with accompanying illustrations.

In the section that follows, we'll look at the key terms and ideas that followed from these first forays into dialect geography.

2.1 Key Concepts from Traditional Dialectology

As Chambers and Trudgill (1980) explain, maps of linguistic features can function as either display maps or interpretive maps (p. 25), both of which do what their names suggest. Display maps are made by assigning the appropriate latitude and longitude to individual responses and then placing those responses on a map for display purposes only, no additional explication or analysis involved. Interpretive maps include additional, analysis-based information. For example, an interpretive map then can demonstrate the presence of an isogloss (the limit of occurrence of an individual linguistic feature), which in turn can be compiled with additional isoglosses to demarcate dialect boundaries. As a quick illustration, let's look at some maps from the North American venture into dialect geography, the Linguistic Atlas Project (LAP). Figure 4 contains two display maps, one for *bunk* (a) and one for *pallet* (b), two of the responses given as terms for a bed made up on the floor for guests.

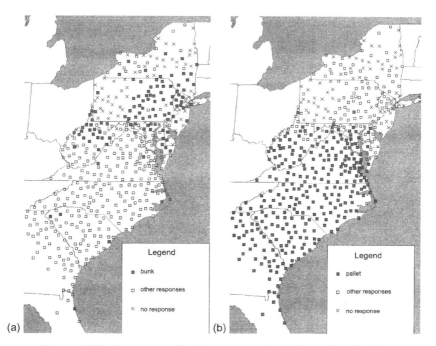

Figure 4 Display maps of LAP responses *bunk* (a) and *pallet* (b).

The maps in Figure 4 contain shaded squares to indicate locations where speakers who were part of the project used each term. Looking at these maps we can observe that *bunk* appears mainly in the northern region of the eastern US and *pallet* occurs in the mid-Atlantic and southern regions, a good example of complementary distribution in which two features appear to have "opposite" regional distributions. Moving into the realm of interpretation, we can add a line to each map that acts as a generalization of these observations. Figure 5 contains the same maps for *bunk* and *pallet*, but in this set of maps, an isogloss has been added that shows the line between "where most people used this term" and "where most people used a different term." This line is supposed to mark where people stop saying one thing (such as *bunk*) and start saying something else (*pallet*). But as we can see, especially in the map for *bunk*, there are occurrences of the term being displayed that fall outside of the cordoned-off region; that is, there are instances of *bunk* in Virginia, North Carolina, South Carolina, and Florida, all of which are considered "southern" states.

For a map with a single isogloss, a dialect cartographer makes decisions about what shaded squares to include within the limit of an isogloss (and which ones to basically ignore). A map with multiple isoglosses that appear to run

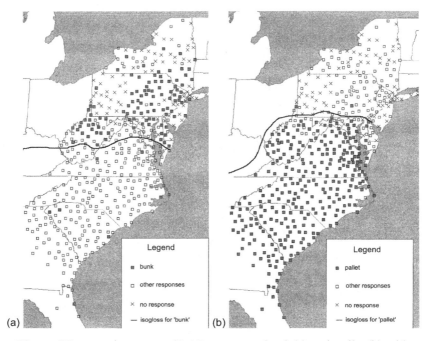

Figure 5 Interpretive maps of LAP responses *bunk* (a) and *pallet* (b) with isoglosses.

together (sometimes referred to as a bundle of isoglosses) can be used to extrapolate a dialect boundary. The idea is that dialects share not just one feature, but a bundle of features that "go together" to form the unique combination that sets one dialect off from another.[5]

A comparison of the distributions *bunk* and *pallet* in Figures 4 and 5 demonstrates that there is a great deal of overlap in terms of where people use which variant; speakers from West Virginia, Delaware, and Maryland have both terms at their disposal. Overlaps such as this are referred to as transition zones, the idea being that the speech of geographic areas adjacent to dialect boundary lines can (and most likely will) contain features associated with the regional dialect on each side of the zone. As the existence of something called a "transition zone" might suggest, isoglosses and dialect boundary lines are not absolute dividing lines. Today's dialect geographers are well aware that these lines "represent a very abstract conceptualization of the way in which dialect regions meet" (Chambers & Trudgill 1980, p. 104). Discussions of transition zones are a good reminder that whenever people interact with each other, no matter what the topic(s) of conversation, it's not just interlocutors' ideas about the conversation content that are being shared; linguistic information is also being exchanged. As Chambers and Trudgill remark, "In order for dialect regions to abut as abruptly as the isogloss implies, they would have to be separated by an unbridgeable abyss" (1980, p. 104).

In fact, the maps for *bunk* and *pallet* are (in a way) rather misleading. Very few LAP variants show as clear-cut a distributional pattern as these two terms; even fewer demonstrate what appears to be a north/south distinction (no matter what popular perceptions of speech in the United States suggest). Additional examples of LAP data, mapped and otherwise, will be presented after a brief history of American dialect geography.

3 American Dialect Geography

Around the same time the first of the Swiss and Italian volumes were published, American linguists were joining the cartographic fraternity. Late in the summer of 1929, a group of American linguists, members of the American Dialect Society (ADS), convened to discuss the possibility of creating an American Linguistic Atlas, modeled on the language maps made in Europe. The scholar chosen to head up the project was Austrian-American linguist Hans Kurath, who led the LAP first from Brown University and then from the University of Michigan for almost twenty years. Kurath wrote reports on the development and

---

[5] As we look more closely at the LAP, we'll see that interpretation gets a bit trickier as more isoglosses are added.

progress of the American dialect project for the ADS publication *Dialect Notes*, sharing what he felt were the pertinent details of the previous years' meetings, agreements, and progress. Before undertaking their own atlas, the American dialectologists sought advice from their European counterparts; Kurath met with Jaberg and Jud to talk about the practicalities of mapping speech, such as how to represent social elements on a map, what size maps should be in order to avoid overcrowding, and so on, as well as the mechanical aspects of the interviews themselves. After meeting with the Swiss dialect geographers, Kurath was clearly heartened, including in the *Notes* for that year that, "perhaps the most important outcome of my interviews [with Jaberg and Jud] is an increased conviction that our project is of the greatest importance, and an increased confidence in our ability to carry it out successfully" (1930, p. 74). It's not often that one witnesses unbridled optimism in an academic, but it seems almost necessary to attain this level of enthusiasm when faced with a task as momentous as carrying out a survey of American English.

The first step in the undertaking of the American atlas was the development of the tool by which linguistic information could be collected and the protocols by which interviews would be conducted. When I was in grad school, I was taught that Kurath himself assembled the list of items and the questions used to elicit them, but it turns out that the process of crafting the worksheets was a bit more complicated. In his 1931 *Dialect Notes* report, Kurath wrote about the questionnaire, explaining first that it would heretofore be referred to as "work sheets" to avoid, as he penned somehow unironically, "the *odium pedagogicum*" of referring to them otherwise (p. 93). Kurath took suggestions mailed in by ADS members on postcards or previously published in the *Notes* word lists. He cycled through several versions of the worksheets, cutting some questions and adding others (see Figure 6). A quick glance at the different versions of the original pages highlights this process of paring down and building back up, illustrating that the worksheets (like most well-researched academic projects) were very much the product of collaboration and revision.

Jud came back to the US during the summer before the American fieldwork started, bringing one of his own fieldworkers to help train the LAP interviewers. They demonstrated the technique they had employed for the Swiss and Italian interviews, turning the daily Atlas staff meetings into a linguistics bootcamp. The fieldworkers-to-be listened to phonograph records of American speakers and transcribed the recorded speech into IPA. Then, as Kurath explained, "the transcriptions were compared, sound for sound, and were discussed fully; and after the criticisms of divergencies, the records were played again." As truly horrifying as that sounds in terms of pressure to perform, this kind of exercise was intended to calibrate the fieldworkers' transcriptions. The goal was

6

```
1        heavy rain    /of short duration/
         goose-drownder, cloudburst,
         down-pour, down-fall, squall

2          thunder storm
         thunder shower, tempest, storm

3        ~~the wind blew hard~~          3     it)blew(all night),it blew and
         blowed                               blew
                                        4     a)the wind's)from the south
✗ 5      a) it's) drizzling                   to the south(w)ard
         splitting                      b) a southwest wind; southeast wind
         b) a steady drizzle            sou(th)wester, southeaster
6        fog                            northeast, northwest

7        foggy
✗ 8      it's) burned off
                                   7

1        drought
         drouth ,dry spell

2          the wind is) picking up
         breezing on, breezing up fresh,
         getting stronger, rising, raising, gusting, coming up,
         blowing higher
3          it's) letting up        a)of a strong wind
         laying, going down        b)of a light wind, a breeze
         dying down, easing up
✗ 4      it's) rather snappy (this morning
         sharp, edgy, keen,fresh, airish

5          we had a) frost
         a freeze
                                    first thin ice
6        a)  the lake) froze over (last night
         friz
✗ b)     it's)frozen (solid
7          sitting room  /where guests are entertained/
         big house, front room,
         parlor, living room, best room

8        the room is) nine foot high
    feet, roots

                         p.7A
   / Make a floor plan of the house and name the rooms/
                         [GSL didwt] '.
```

Figure 6 Handwritten notes on Kurath's original worksheets.

uniformity across fieldworkers' representations of speech in order to ensure that, in later comparisons of the speech of one place to another, the differences would truly be differences, and not the product of fieldworker idiosyncrasies.[6] They also practiced "live" interviews, again under scrutiny, to ensure an evenness across interviewers.[7] The LAP fieldworkers began interviewing speakers

---

[6] But of course there were differences, including one fieldworker's intense fondness for the IPA symbol referred to as a "barred I."

[7] Again there were differences; Raven McDavid was what we'd now refer to as a "foodie" and would ask (in)famously lengthy and detailed follow-up questions for food items.

```
                                          8
✗1        picture
 2        a) chimney

          b) hearth                    3  and irons

 3        mantlexshelf the lamp,etc, is on the) mantle shelf
          mantle piece, mantle, tussock, clock shelf, fire board

✗4        chimney  /of an industrial plant/
          smoke stack

 5        a) log
   ✗b)     chunk /split wood for stove/  billet,stick
 6         soot

 7        a) the ashes are (white                              Ᵹ
          is
          b) it burns to ) white ashes , a white ash
 8         chair

                                          9

 1         sofa
          lounge, couch
 2        chest of drawers  /describe!/
          dresser, bureau

 3        whatxiexaxxxxxxxxxxxxxxxxxxxxxxxxxxxxxxxxxx  3   furniture
                                                          house fixings,
 ✗ 4       bedroom                   plunder now plunder, tricks
          chamber, sleeping house

 5        window shades  /roller shades/
          blinds, curtains

 6        a) clothes closet /built in/        b)      wardrobe
          clothes press, closet, press               wardroom
 7         garret
          attic, sky-parlor, cock loft

 8        kitchen /describe/
          porch, cook room , kitchen house
          cook house

 ✗ 9       summer kitchen
          cellar kitchen
```

Figure 6 (cont.)

for the Linguistic Atlas of New England (LANE) in the early 1930s. It took the team of nine fieldworkers three years to complete 416 interviews across the region. Each interview lasted between six and ten hours, as the fieldworker took the informant through about 100 pages worth of targeted questions.[8]

---

[8] Several critiques of Atlas methods (e.g. Pickford 1956, Alexander 1940, Peyt 1980) noted that the interviews were so long that one informant actually died during the course of the interview. This is true, though it should also be noted that the interviews often took place over the course of several days and, in this poor fellow's case, his brand-new widow felt that the project was important enough for her to offer to complete the final pages of questions herself, presumably only days after her husband died.

In addition to writing down speakers' answers to the survey questions in IPA, portions of some of the interviews were recorded via phonograph, as described in a *Dialect Notes* entry: "a portable recording set, which can be operated either from alternating current or from batteries, makes it possible to record any-where." The novelty of this situation is emphasized in an addendum to the *Notes*, written by one of the LANE fieldworkers, Miles Hanley, who explained, "permanent electrical recordings of good quality are being made *in the homes* of the speakers" (1933, p. 368) Those are his italics, which shows that being able to record someone outside of a studio setting must have seemed fantastical, almost as amazing as having those recordings survive to the present day. One set of the resulting aluminum discs is housed in the Library of Congress; the other lives in the University of Kentucky Special Collections Research Center. As one can imagine, the sound quality of the original disks isn't great, but there's something otherworldly about listening to the voices of everyday people who agreed to help out traveling linguists almost 100 years ago.

After the New England survey was completed, the next regional survey was the Linguistic Atlas of the Middle and South Atlantic States (LAMSAS). The principal LAMSAS fieldworkers, Raven McDavid and Guy Lowman, talked to over 1,100 people over the course of the 1930s and 1940s all along the east coast, from New York state to northern Florida. Included in this second spate of regional interviews were interviews conducted by Lorenzo Dow Turner, the first African American to earn a PhD in Linguistics. Turner interviewed twenty-one speakers of Gullah who lived on the Sea Islands off the coasts of South Carolina and Georgia. Linguists had been anxious to collect samples of Gullah, which to date is the only agreed-upon English-based creole spoken in the contiguous United States, but it wasn't until Turner approached the communities that the Gullah speakers were willing to speak to an outsider.

Within the early LAP surveys, there isn't much data from women or minority speakers. The early interviewees tilted toward the "N.O.R.M." – nonmobile older rural (white) male.[9] One of the reasons there were so few women interviewed in the 1930s and 1940s was that it would have been viewed as inappropriate for a male interviewer to spend that much time with another man's wife (which might also explain why many of the women who were interviewed were widows or elderly singles). There aren't that many women among the early LANE or LAMSAS interviewees and part of the reason was that there was only a handful of women who worked on the project in those days; Rachel Harris was a LANE field-worker who conducted forty-nine interviews, and Marguerite Chapallaz, a phonetician from London, conducted thirteen interviewed and then worked

---

[9] Another acronym is W.O.R.M. (white, older, rural male).

with everyone's data after it was collected. Later, during the LAMSAS era, Virginia McDavid (wife of Raven) did an enormous amount of work with the LAMSAS worksheets and published seminal works on the dialects of American English, both with her husband and on her own. It's also the case that people don't necessarily like to talk openly with someone they don't feel comfortable with; one can only imagine what a rural farming community made of a tweed-jacketed phonograph-toting stranger who breezes into town and wants to spend a couple of afternoons asking people hundreds of questions. Turner was able to gain access to the Gullah community because he was patient and persistent, but it helped that he, too, was Black. In a perfect world, we'd have more voices represented, and we do see this happen as later surveys get less NORM-al and more demographically well-rounded.

By the end of 1933, after LANE was completed and sample interviews had been conducted in other areas. Turner had completed his Gullah interviews. Atlas headquarters was a busy hive of scholars working to compile the biographies of the informants, doing phonetic analyses, charting individual items, and sorting question responses into social groups. Editorial procedure solidified, and an Index was prepared. It was time to make some maps. In his *Dialect Notes* remarks, Kurath reports that there was some debate as to what color the topographical background of the map should be (various shades of green, brown, and gray were tested) until light green was chosen as "the most satisfactory color, since it allows the black lines of linguistic entries to stand out most clearly against the lines of the map,"[10] but he adds that "various questions of format and size are still under discussion." In the end, over 700 maps were prepared and published in three volumes: one set of books containing maps that are 2 × 3 feet, and one set with maps that are 3 × 5 feet (i.e., sizes "large" and "larger").

3.1 The LAP Regional Surveys

In the *Foreward* to the LANE volumes, written by later linguists, the atlas as conceived by Kurath is described as having been "heroically designed"; the kind of expansive, comprehensive study of American English dialects that Kurath agreed to undertake must necessarily be carried out in stages. And indeed, Kurath's heroic efforts served as the foundation for efforts to come as additional regional surveys followed LANE and LAMSAS, steered first by Kurath's students and then Raven McDavid's, and, for the most part, each new regional survey used the same set of interview questions. Thus the present-day LAP materials comprise data (collected on paper or via audio recordings)

---

[10] Some of the published maps have a green background, but some are light tan.

from a series of discrete yet related regional LAP surveys. Following LANE and LAMSAS came the Linguistic Atlas of the North Central States (LANCS) and the Linguistic Atlas of the Pacific Coast (LAPC) – both of these are contemporaries of LAMSAS though their data are (at the moment) less fully explored. Another behemoth of a survey, directed by Lee Pederson, is the Linguistic Atlas of the Gulf States (LAGS), which includes interview data from 914 speakers from Florida, Georgia, Tennessee, Alabama, Mississippi, Louisiana, Arkansas, and Texas, interviewed between 1968 and 1983. A quick reference to all of the LAP surveys is presented in Table 1. All told, the LAP contains data from about 5500 speakers, mostly from the 1930s through the 1960s, although interviews as recent as 2004 have been conducted. To this day, the LAP remains the largest and most comprehensive survey of American English ever undertaken.

3.2 Kurath's Dialect Boundaries

Data from the first two regional surveys, LANE and LAMSAS, were the basis of the first Atlas Project dialect maps, published in Kurath's 1949 *Word Geography of the Eastern United States*. The *Word Geography* was focused on the regional distribution of lexical items with an eye toward those that seemed to cluster around a specific region or subregion and the best way to do this is to create (what would have been physical) maps of individual words. After individual variants for lexical targets were mapped, Kurath drew isoglosses, and where several isoglosses ran concurrently, he drew a dialect boundary. Kurath commented on the use of isoglosses to indicate dialect areas on a map:

> Speech areas, large and small, can be "spotted" by selecting representative isoglosses from the available examples. This convenient device is employed throughout this [work] to delineate in a simplified manner the dialectal structure of the Eastern States insofar as it is revealed in the everyday vocabulary. In most cases, the word lines are chosen to exhibit the focus or "core" of an area as well as its periphery or margin. One must, of course, keep in mind that this procedure does not tell the whole story. The full complexity of regional and local usage is displayed in the Linguistic Atlas itself. (Kurath 1949, p. 11)

Kurath himself noted that maps with word lines (a phrase that absolutely should be brought back into dialectological parlance as a synonym of "isogloss") are only "part of the story"; the maps featured in the *Word Geography* represent "core" lexical items that were elicited from large numbers of speakers in a particular area. For each of the dialect-determining targets, there are a great many variants given as a response by only a few speakers

Table 1 Reference to the LAP regional surveys.

Survey	Director(s)	Interview dates	States	# Speakers	Audio?
Linguistic Atlas of New England (LANE)	H. Kurath	1931–1933	MA, NH, CT, VT, NY, RI, ME	416	Y (partial interviews have been transcribed)
Linguistic Atlas of the Middle and South Atlantic States (LAMSAS)	H. Kurath	1933–1974	NY, NJ, PA, WV, DE, MD, VA, NC, SC, GA, FL	1162	Some
Linguistic Atlas of the North Central States (LANCS)	A. Marckwardt	1933–1978	WI, MI, IL, IN, OH, KY	542	Some (transcription of full interviews underway)
Linguistic Atlas of the Gulf States (LAGS)	L. Pederson	1968–1983	FL, GA, TN, AL, MS, LA, AR, TX	914	Y
Linguistic Atlas of Oklahoma (LAO)	W. Van Riper	1960–1962	OK	57	Y
Linguistic Atlas of the Pacific Northwest (LAPNW)	C. Reed D. Carlson		OR, WA, ID	51	Some
Linguistic Atlas of the Pacific Coast (LAPC)	D. Reed A. Metcalf	1952–1959	CA, NV	300	N

					Y (interviews fully transcribed)
Linguistic Atlas of the Middle Rockies (LAMR) ́	L. Pederson, L. Antieau	1988–2004	CO, WY, UT	70	
Linguistic Atlas of the Upper Midwest (LAUM)	H. Allen M. Linn	1949–1962	MN, IA, ND, SD, NE	203	N
Georgia Dialect Survey (GDS)	L. Pederson	1968–1972	GA	288	Y
Linguistic Survey of Louisiana (LSL)	C.M. Wise	1935–1951	LA	84	N
Linguistic Atlas of Hawai'i (LAH)	C.M. Wise	1950	HI	8	N
Gullah	L.D. Turner	1933	SC, GA	21	Unsure
St. Kitts Nevis Project (SKNP)	L. Pederson	2003	St. Kitts, Nevis	23	Y
Linguistic Atlas of Southern England (LASE)	G. Lowman	1937–1938	Southern England	59	N
Hudson Valley (HuVa)	J. Hawkins	1938–1940	NY, NJ	34	N

and these responses don't show up on the *Word Geography* display maps; this is likely the "full complexity" to which Kurath refers. One doesn't have to spend a lot of time with the full Atlas datasets to realize that variation in language goes way beyond choices between two (or three, or ten) options. In fact, for many of the LAP prompts, there were dozens, if not hundreds, of variants produced; in addition, most speakers were themselves familiar with multiple terms for many linguistic targets.

For the variants that were "spotted" as having regional salience, the *Word Geography* includes interpretive maps with their generalized area occurrence marked with an isogloss. Figure 7 contains the individual isoglosses for

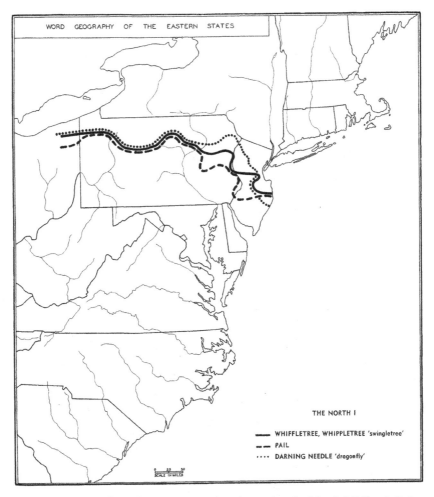

Figure 7 The bundle of isoglosses used to determine the North Midland dialect boundary line (from Kurath 1949, fig. 5a).

whiffletree/whippletree (names for the crossbar on an animal-drawn wagon or plow), *pail*, and *darning needle* (a variant of "dragonfly"), which were common responses of LAP informants who lived north of the lines. The distribution of these responses was then used to determine the southernmost boundary of the Northern dialect region, the idea being that below this boundary, speakers used different variants for the three targets in question.

The Midland dialect region boundary lines were determined by different variants and/or targets. Figure 8 contains the map with isoglosses used to cordon

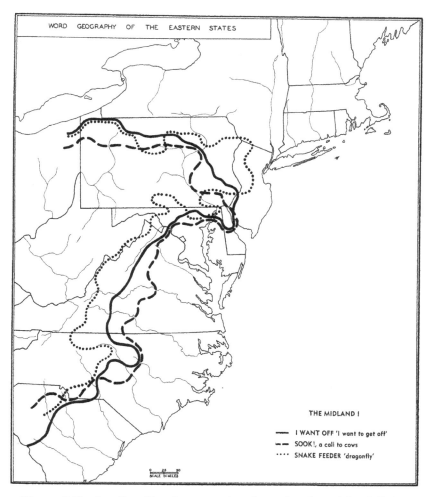

Figure 8 The bundle of isoglosses used to determine the Midland dialect boundary lines (from Kurath 1949, fig. 15).

off the Midland from both the Northern and Southern dialect regions: *I want off* for 'I want to get off [of a ride]', *sook!* as a call to cows, and *snake feeder* for "dragonfly." The lines on this map make an elbow-bend in Delaware; *snake feeder* twists and turns through Pennsylvania, New Jersey, and Virginia, but despite slight meanderings of individual lines, these three isoglosses travel together, suggesting that these specific lexical items differentiate Midland from the North and also from the South.

We see another combination of targets and variants in Figure 9, which contains the isoglosses for the items deemed to distinguish the Southern dialect

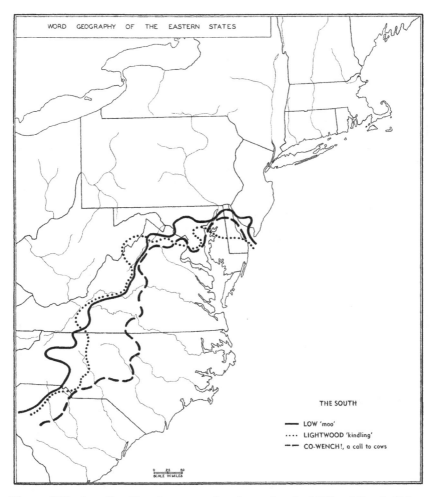

Figure 9 The bundle of isoglosses used to determine the Midland South dialect boundary line (from Kurath 1949, fig. 29).

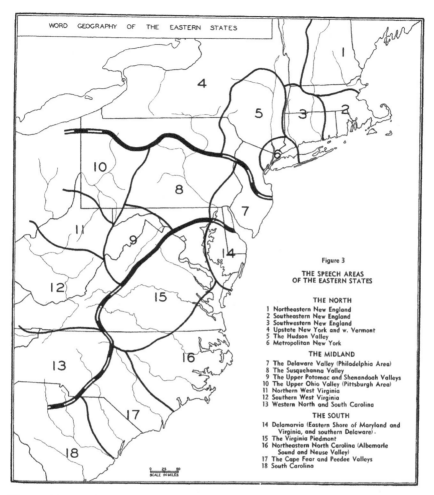

Figure 10 Kurath's map of the Northern, Midland, and Southern dialect regions
(from Kurath 1949, fig 5).

boundary: *low* as the term for a cow's moo, *lightwood* for "kindling," and *co-wench!* as a call to cows. Taken together, the sets of isoglosses presented in the maps of Figures 7, 8, and 9 were generalized to form three major dialect boundaries, illustrated here as Figure 10, a stylized version of Kurath's original map.

Following up on the discussion of isoglosses and boundary lines from Section 2.1, it is important to note that Kurath used what we would now call a "best fit" method for drawing dialect boundaries. He took some editorial

license as he smoothed over inconsistencies and geographic outliers and cer-
tainly took liberties in choosing representative features whose distributions
reflected where he thought the dialect boundary lines should run
(Kretzschmar 2003, p. 134). This is not a criticism of Kurath or his mapping
techniques – we call these "interpretive maps" for a reason – but instead as
a reminder that mapping is a "theory-driven enterprise" (Kretzschmar 2003,
p. 130), which means that lines on a map are motivated by the map-drawer's
knowledge, assumptions, and beliefs. In this case, Kurath's knowledge of
settlement patterns and migration routes influenced where the boundaries
ran.[11] The boundary between the Midland and the North, for example, follows
the Great Wagon Road westward, and the boundary between the Midland and
the South mirrors a major migration route from eastern Pennsylvania southward
through the Shenandoah River Valley.

Though there have been a series of updated and expanded US dialect maps
produced by linguists since the 1940s – ones informed by phonological or
grammatical data and/or ones whose lines move further west – the basic
demarcations made by Kurath have stood the test of time. (And, in this author's
humble opinion, they have done so because Kurath's maps have always been
interdisciplinary in nature, i.e., they have always taken into consideration
cultural factors in addition to recorded language use.)

3.3 Update on LAP Status

Right now, "heroic" describes the tasks set before today's Atlas team as most
of the LAP data sits in 600+ acid-free boxes awaiting exploration. The boxes
offer a cornucopia of media upon which Atlas data is stored; we have paper
(lots of paper),[12] microfiche, aluminum discs, cassette tapes, reel-to-reel
recordings, and even twelve boxes of gold CDs. When people come to visit
the Atlas office, a common exclamation is that they feel "overwhelmed" and it
is a bit daunting to see boxes lining the walls, seven boxes high, but the LAP
offers sociolinguistic researchers the opportunity of a lifetime.

The LAP holdings aren't just "research," however; the boxes of hand-bound
notebooks and folders represent the people who gave their time and their words
to a stranger – people who have long since passed away, and whose grandchil-
dren and great-grandchildren might not even know that their Papaw or Granny

---

[11] Settlement patterns and migration routes are appropriate touchstones for dialect boundary-
drawing given that these are two of the historical forces that led to the creation of dialects in
the Eastern US to begin with, a theory perhaps most fully articulated by Raven McDavid's
chapter in W. Nelson Francis' *The Structure of American English* 1958b.

[12] So much paper.

did something special and something important for the study of dialects in the United States. The boxes that line the Atlas office walls also represent the efforts of dozens of fieldworkers who studied, bootcamped, trained, and traveled across the United States to be of service to something larger than themselves. Add to this the countless hours spent by the Atlas team back at various home-bases in academic offices, proofreading, correcting, tallying, counting, and mapping. Taken together, the Atlas materials are a physical manifestation of an enormous effort made by real people who believed in being a part of a project they took to heart as being valuable and worthwhile. What follows is a deeper dive into the inner workings of the LAP, starting with a look at the Atlas interview.

4 The Atlas Interview

After completing intensive training, a small cadre of Atlas fieldworkers spread out across the rural areas of New England in 1931, the first team to undertake what would be many decades' worth of LAP interviews. The fieldworkers were given a charge by the LAP director himself, and Kurath's handwritten instructions began with the sage warning:

> Beware preconceived notions. Do not be misled by what you know, but trust your ear and eye. Rejoice in discovering new facts, and in having your expectations disappointed. Alertness and keenness of perception are the important factors for this work.

The idea that one should "rejoice in being disappointed" is a good reminder that when things don't go as expected, look around for the thing that you learned that's new and what you found that you didn't expect to find. At the outset of their quest to find these new facts, the Atlas fieldworkers were equipped with "special blank books of bond paper" and "first-class thin carbon paper" so the fieldnotes would be made in duplicate,[13] which only partially explains why the Atlas boxes are filled with so much paper.[14] It was also recommended that they take with them a small journal for making notes-to-self and for jotting down the biographical information gathered from each informant, which would note their occupation, their age, where they were born, where their parents and grandparents were from, and the amount of schooling they had undertaken.

---

[13] For younger readers, carbon paper was placed in between pages so that what was written on the top page was pressed onto the bottom page: the original "cc" for "carbon copy."

[14] That and the fact that in one box there was a folder with – no lie – *dozens* of drafts of the same pages on topographical features, both handwritten versions and typed versions with handwritten corrections.

4.1 Informant Bios and Character Sketches

After the early LAP interviews, fieldworkers would add to the biographical overview of each informant a brief "character sketch," which was basically the fieldworker's impression of the personality and language of the speaker, to include their "alertness and intelligence, extent and accuracy of information, attitude toward the investigator and his task, naturalness or guardedness in utterance, interest in 'improving' the language." Many of these biographical vignettes are gems, singing with personality and no small amount of (perhaps unintended) humor. Among the LANE and LAMSAS informant bios, we find descriptors such as "strikingly handsome," "first rate informant," "loquacious on a variety of irrelevant subjects," and "kind, affable, glad to be of help." What follows are a few additional examples of LAP character sketches (with family info removed).[15]

> WV37B! F, 69, spinster, b[orn in] same house. [. . .] Southern Methodist – Somewhat prim and self-conscious, essentially a local cultivated type. Interested in traditions but unimpressed by the importance of the study.
> SC25A F, housewife, 78. [. . .] Baptist. – Sat puffing away at her pipe, enjoying the questionnaire from beginning to end. Composed, companionable; a sparkle of Irish wit. – Not at all guarded about her speech; speech is quaintly antique and vulgar. Slow speech, long vowels. Nasal in the vicinity of nasal vowels.
> CT283: M, fisherman, 68. [. . .] 2 years of high school – Spends most of his time on the water; has always been an outdoor man. Methodist. Tall, powerful, proud of his health and strength. Stern moral principles. Loud, penetrating, rather raucous voice. Frequently uses a velarized *r* which sounds like a uvular fricative.

As it turns out, the published LANE and LAMSAS character sketches were highly edited. Recently, the Atlas team has discovered handwritten, unedited versions of character sketches, which are currently being considered as another form of "Atlas data" (this new approach will be discussed in detail Section 6.3.3).

4.2 Interview Targets

There were over 800 targets that fieldworkers were trained to elicit with questions that provided a description or context and asked the interviewee to fill in the

---

[15] The alphanumeric codes are the LAP "informant numbers" composed of state abbreviations plus a community number and (maybe) an "A," "B," "C," etc. if there was more than one speaker interviewed in that community. An exclamation point ("!") indicated that the informant was considered "cultured" by the fieldworker. The letters "N" and "M" were used to indicate that an informant was African American ("N" was for "Negro").

blank. The Atlas targets can be thought of as individual linguistic items; mostly lexical, although there were plenty of pronunciation targets along with a number of questions aimed at collecting variation in the articulation of grammatical constructions as well. A handful of examples, along with their target in [brackets] follow. Note that some targets did double-duty as both a lexical and pronunciation target (like "fog") or as both a grammatical and pronunciation target (like "ride").

- Lexical targets
  - Sometimes you make up a batter and fry three or four of these at a time. You eat them with syrup and butter. What would you call these? [pancakes]
  - Room at the top of the house just under the roof. [attic]
  - The kind of black and white animal with a powerful smell. Other names? [skunk]
  - If it's been fair and then the clouds come and you expect rain or snow in a little while, you say the weather is ____. [threatening]
- Pronunciation targets
  - Sometimes you feel you get your good luck just a little at a time, but your bad luck comes _____. [all at once]
  - What do you call the heavy white mist that comes out of the river? [fog]
  - What's left in the fireplace when the fire goes out? If someone asks you the color, you would say ____. [white ashes]
- Grammatical targets
  - What time did the sun rise this morning? You say the sun ____ at six. [rose]
  - If it's 10:45, what time do you say it is? [quarter till/quarter to]
  - If no one will do it for him, you say he had better do it _____. [himself]
  - Everyone around here likes to ___ horses; last year he ___ his every morning. [ride, rode]

The fieldworkers had a set list of questions, but again, they still had their own style. For example, the questions used to elicit terms for a porch (e.g., *piazza, stoop, veranda,* etc.) were these:

  - What is built outside the door to walk on and put chairs on? What do you call the little one just over the door? [porch]

Fieldworker Guy Lowman stopped here; Raven McDavid did not. He often had follow-up questions, and the "porch" question is a good example of how he liked to probe for more information.

  - What would you call one that was big and had columns on it? What would you call one that ran around the front and side of the house? Can you have a porch with more than one floor? What do you call the one up-stairs? What do you call the one at the back of the house? Does it make any difference if it has a roof?

Though not all fieldworkers asked such extensive follow-up questions, they would make notes about what speakers said a specific word referred to. For instance, if someone said that they felt that "porch" and "veranda" were pretty much the same thing, it was noted. Thus, the LAP field notebook pages give us a glimpse into the lexicon (the mental dictionary) of people from a specific time and place.

While these questions may seem like they would create a choppy back-and-forth between the fieldworker and informant, the Atlas interviews were still very much a conversation. The fieldworkers weren't simply "butterfly collecting" – they weren't just gathering words and phrases to pin to a shadowbox somewhere – they were also asking follow-up questions to try to understand the contexts in which people used the terms that they did. Was the word old-fashioned or modern? Had they heard other words for the same thing? What's the difference between the things that these words represent? When you roll it all together, each speaker's answers are a detailed portrait of that individual and about what life was like in that place at that point in time, which means that there's a lot of cultural information folded into the Atlas notebook pages.

4.3 Anatomy of a Worksheet

The result of hours of questions is pages and pages of answers. The notebooks used by the fieldworkers to record the responses for each targeted question (in duplicate) were stamped on every page with the informant number, so that, when the pages were unbound (and then sometimes rebound), you could keep track of who gave what responses to each question. Items on these pages were grouped (sort of) thematically, so one finds a page with a lot of furniture-related or kitchen-related items on it. Target items are referred to by page number and item number; for example, the target item "bureau" is the second item on page nine, so we'd say "bureau" is target 9.2.

Figure 11 is a page from one of the LAMSAS field notebooks from the interview with informant number "VA38," which you can see is labeled in the top right corner as page "9." The left-hand column contains the responses that VA38 (a white 43-year-old man who worked as a Navy Yard clerk) gave to questions about what terms he used for "sofa," "dresser," "furniture," and so on. The right-hand side of the page is the comment column, which is where the fieldworker could add extra information. On this page, we see that VA38 had three

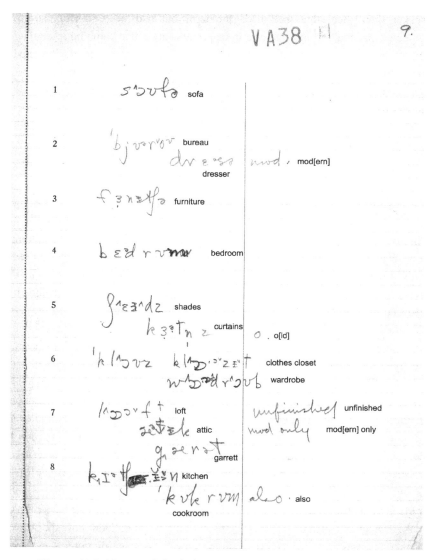

Figure 11 LAP page 9 for informant VA38; transcription added for convenience.

different terms for "attic" and that he distinguished between them based on whether or not the space was finished (unfinished means that for VA38, it was a *loft*) or if the term was "modern only" (*attic*). He also used the term *cookroom* for "kitchen." Sometimes the fieldworker would use a comment code: s. ("suggested" which means the fieldworker used the word first), h. ("heard" which indicated that the speaker didn't feel that they used the term but had heard others use it), c. ("conversational" to indicate a term or pronunciation that came up in another part of the interview conversation, as opposed to in answer to the targeted question), o. (for terms that speakers felt were "old" or "old-fashioned"), and mod. (for terms the speaker considered to be "modern"). Bear in mind that the piece of paper featured in Figure 11 is now almost ninety years old; it is the product of an earlier generation, that generation's technology, and its ideas about how best to study the language that real people use.

4.4 Page 7a

The "words and things" movement of Europe remained a subtle undercurrent throughout the Atlas surveys to the extent that, every now and then, a fieldworker would make a quick sketch of a piece of furniture or the shape of a haystack to indicate more clearly what a speaker was referring to when using a particular word. Kurath's original instructions for fieldworkers also included a page 7a, which asked interviewers to sketch out a floorplan of informants' homes and label the rooms. Actual examples of a page 7a remained elusive and untouched until recently, but now they have been recovered and the Atlas materials contain page 7a for hundreds of speakers, mostly from LAMSAS and from the LAGS.

Figure 12 contains an example page 7a from SC speaker 6N from 1946, which contains a sketch of the floorplan of a small house with six rooms. The speaker mentions a *front door* and *entryway* that lead to a hall running down the middle of the house. To the left of the hallway, we see three rooms designated as *bedroom*, the last of which is also noted as being the *companying room* (a guest bedroom perhaps?), and the bathroom (referred to as both the *toilet* and the *lavatory*). To the right of the hallway, immediately inside the front door, we see the *setting room* or *living room*, followed by the *dining room* and *kitchen* (located at the back of the house). Diagrams such as this provide us with information about how the Atlas speakers' houses were laid out in addition to what names the different rooms were called, so in comparing these quickly-sketched floorplans we can get an idea of how houses varied from one another in the 1930s and '40s, as well as how room names varied. Note, too, that this SC speaker had more than one term at his disposal for both the third company bedroom and for the setting (living) room.

Investigation of the linguistic and cultural data that can be gleaned from page 7a has only recently begun, but these sketches (along with other sketches found amid the fieldwork pages) offer the opportunity for transdisciplinary investigations into the connections between language and (material) culture.

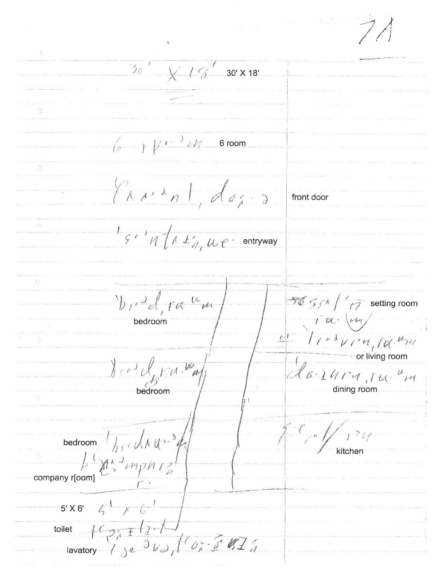

Figure 12 Page 7a for LAP informant SC6N.

5 LAP Language Data

Surveying the whole of LAP data, one encounters a large collection of comparable datasets from regional surveys from across the US, though the degree to which each of the datasets is accessible differs, depending on the specific survey. What this means is that an examination of a specific linguistic feature as it is found across surveys can entail different methods for and amounts of processing for that data to be usable in research projects. Generally speaking, the processing of LAP data begins with transcription. For older LAP data this means transcribing responses recorded in IPA into normal orthography; for more recently collected data this entails transcribing field audio recordings (as one might in contemporary variationist sociolinguistics). Again, these processes yield comparable data, that is, the variants of specific targets, but how those variants can be accessed within individual regional surveys differs, depending on when, where, and how the data was collected. What follows is an overview of what comparable data – specifically, terms given in LAP interviews for "thunderstorm" – look like within representative regional projects.

5.1 LAP Dataset: LANE Example

For the most part, LANE data can be accessed in two ways: by going through the original (or scanned) field pages with responses to the targeted questions recorded in IPA, or by using the LANE maps published between 1939 and 1943.[16] Figure 13 contains images of two LANE field pages, the left one from a Massachusetts speaker (MA153) and the right from a Connecticut speaker (CT282), each of them a page 6. The second target on page 6 (i.e., item 6.2) was "thunderstorm," for which interviewers asked speakers about what they call "a storm with thunder and lightning." On the left, we see the responses *a regular cloudburst* and *thundershower*, while on the right we have *electric storm* and *thundershower*.

The sample LANE pages displayed in Figure 13 represent the responses of just two speakers; over the course of the late 1930s, Kurath and his team compiled LANE speakers' responses to their interview questions to make maps like the one featured in Figure 14. The LANE maps were handmade, originally fashioned by placing individual characters on top of a lithograph map template. The map pages also include a brief commentary and a series of examples; the commentary gives a general picture of the range of responses and their social distribution, and examples appear to have been selected to illustrate (interesting) pronunciations, usages, or evaluations.

Given the commentary provided on map 94, the most frequent terms for "thunderstorm" in the New England territory were *storm, thunderstorm, lightning storm, electric(al) storm, shower, thundershower, electrical shower, tempest*, and *thunder and rain shower*. The commentary also includes jocular terms, some discussion of *storm* versus *shower*, and a paragraph on the use of *tempest* in the New England area.

---

[16] The LANE maps are also now available digitally.

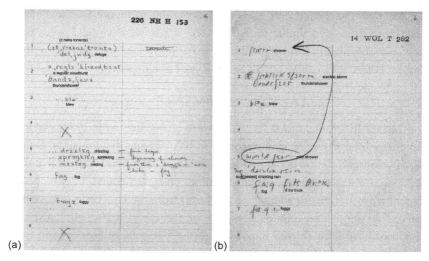

Figure 13 Example LANE field pages with responses to LAP target 6.2 "thunderstorm" (transcriptions provided for convenience).

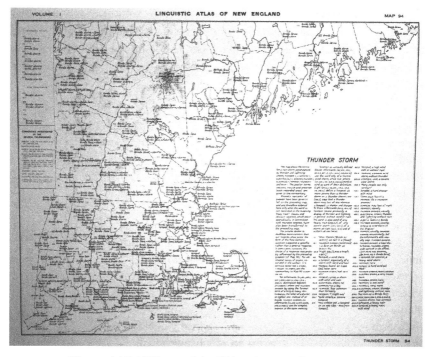

Figure 14 LANE map 94 of "thunderstorm" responses.

Except for the existence of maps such as the one in Figure 14, most of the LAP projects are in a similar state as LANE, where we have field pages with responses recorded in IPA that will need to be transcribed into normal, written English before they can be tallied and analyzed as a dataset.

5.2 LAP Dataset: LAMSAS Example

For the LAMSAS, interviews for which were carried out in the 1930s and 40s, responses to targets were again recorded in IPA on paper field records. Unlike LANE, the transcription of the LAMSAS field records is complete and text files of those transcriptions are available online. Over the course of 30+ years, student workers (undergraduate and graduate) from the University of Georgia worked on these transcriptions, and as of the early 2020s, all LAMSAS responses have been entered into a .csv format. These .csv files contain each LAMSAS informant's response for each target, such that making an ordered list of responses and their frequencies is not difficult.

The LAMSAS response types for "thunderstorm" and their corresponding number of occurrences are given in Table 2. In answer to the "thunderstorm" question, LAMSAS informants gave 1,982 responses comprised of 78 different responses. In technical terms, we'd say that there were 1,982 tokens that represented 78 response types. In addition to the different response types, there were also sixty-two instances in which the question about thunderstorms was not asked (NA) and fifty-two instances in which the question was asked but no response (NR) was given.

Table 2 LAMSAS "thunderstorm" response types and number of tokens.

thunderstorm	804	blow storm	1
thundershower	264	bluster	1
storm	149	breakdown	1
thundercloud	119	cat squall	1
electric storm	89	dust storm	1
thunder gust	76	electricity storm	1
thundersquall	62	fast wind	1
electrical storm	45	fierce thunderstorm	1
tornado	45	flurry of wind	1
squall	44	gale of wind	1
windstorm	44	heavy cloud	1
hurricane	38	heavy squall	1

Table 2 (cont.)

cyclones	37	heavy thundershower	1
gust	26	heavy wind	1
storms	11	lightning and thunder storm	1
thunder and lightning storm	11	rain and wind squall	1
lightning storm	10	right smart thunderstorm	1
twister	10	short thunderstorm	1
rainstorm	9	snow showers	1
hailstorm	6	snow squall	1
thunder	5	squall gale	1
gale	4	squall snap	1
whirlwind	4	steady wind	1
shower	3	strong winds	1
tempest	3	sudden wind	1
thunder and lightning	3	summer shower	1
thunder rain	3	thunder and lightning shower	1
bad cloud	2	thunder and wind storm	1
big storm	2	thunder roll two time	1
flagstorm	2	thundering in the molly hole	1
hard wind	2	tidewater	1
heavy storm	2	torment	1
sandstorm	2	tropical storm	1
snowstorm	2	white squall	1
a east storm	1	wind and rain storm	1
bad storm	1	wind gusts	1
big stormy rain	1	wind squall	1
blinger	1	windfall	1
blizzard	1	yawl	1

The "thunderstorm" dataset from LAMSAS demonstrates, numerically and in a table format, what Kurath (probably) meant when implied a distinction between what one sees as the "core" variants of a target, which are the most frequently given responses to a prompt, and what one sees when the "full complexity" of the LAP is considered. In the case of the data presented in Table 2, the core terms are *thunderstorm, thundershower, storm, thundercloud* (just to take those that were given as responses over 100 times), while the other seventy-four responses, many of which were given as a response only one or two times, are the ones that "flesh out" the full set of data.

"Thunderstorm" responses are a particularly interesting set of data due to the geographic distribution of the different response types. Because each response is associated with an informant number in the .csv file and we have detailed databases that include the latitude and longitude for each informant's community, creating maps of individual response types is relatively easy as well. Figure 15 contains example display maps of the "thunderstorm" variants: *thundershower, electric(al) storm, thundersquall, thunder gust,* and *thundercloud.*

Figure 15 Display maps of "thunderstorm" variants, from top to bottom: *thundershower, electric(al) storm, thundersquall.*

Figure 15 continued: *thunder gust* (top) and *thundercloud* (bottom)

If you compare the distribution of these terms in Figure 15 with the dialect boundaries of Figure 10, you'll notice that none of the "thunderstorm" variants featured above can be characterized as belonging to any of Kurath's dialect regions – there are other types of distribution, some "explainable," some not. *Thundershower*, for instance, has a fairly even distribution across the LAMSAS area, with a small cluster in New Jersey and a scarcity in central and coastal North Carolina and central Virginia, where another term was preferred. *Electric(al) storm* and has an unusual distribution, which, at first glance, appears to be the result of what we would call a fieldworker effect. A single LAMSAS fieldworker, Raven McDavid, conducted 278 interviews with speakers in New York, South Carolina, and Georgia, and sometimes, when you see a term that only occurs in the northernmost and southernmost portions of the LAMSAS territory (and not used at all in the middle), it's the result of McDavid's interview style (i.e., the use of follow-up questions) that often resulted in more variants per speaker than is found in the interview data collected by Guy Lowman. The fieldworker effect does not, however, explain the distribution of *electric(al) storm*, as one can see the dots travel down the Appalachian

Mountains before pooling in South Carolina and Georgia. *Thundersquall* occurs almost exclusively on the coast, which makes sense as *squall* is a nautical term for a storm at sea. The response *thunder gust* occurs only seventy-six times and these occurrences are clustered mainly in the Chesapeake Bay area. Finally, *thundercloud* occurs mainly in eastern Virginia and North Carolina, in complement to *thundershower*. These distributions don't follow Kurath's dialect boundary lines, but instead form their own pattern of localized use.

5.3 LAP Dataset: LAGS Example

Like LAMSAS, the individual LAGS responses for each LAP target have already been transcribed into regular orthography, but unlike LAMSAS, the initial transcriptions were carried out in the late 1970s and then stored with an unreadable file extension; it wasn't until early 2022 that the LAGS text file "puzzle" was solved and the files made usable again. Table 3 contains the LAGS responses for the "thunderstorm" question, 981 tokens comprised of 47 response types.

Because the core of the LAP interview has persisted, comparisons can be made across regional surveys.

For example, the order, by frequency, of variants in LAGS differs from that of LAMSAS and it is these differences that one can use to carry out comparisons – between geographical regions or between time periods.

Table 3 LAGS "thunderstorm" response types and number of tokens.

thunderstorm	383	bad cloud	1
electrical storm	166	bad rain	1
storm	153	banshee	1
electric storm	83	bluster	1
thundershower	43	blustery weather	1
lightning storm	31	devil's tossing watermelons	1
rainstorm	17	drum a-beating	1
windstorm	14	electrical cloud	1
stormy weather	11	equinox storm	1
cloudburst	8	good blow	1
stormy	8	lot of thunder and lightning	1
thundercloud	7	northeaster storm	1
bad weather	5	rough weather	1
bad storm	4	severe storm	1
electrical	4	storm cloud	1

addition to maps, these publications contained dialect checklists indicating what words and pronunciations were used to determine dialect boundaries.

In addition to studies of lexical features, scholarly investigations of Atlas data during this era included discussion of the distribution – social as well as geographic – of grammatical features (e.g., Atwood 1953, V. McDavid 1956) and pronunciation (Kurath & R. McDavid 1961). Raven McDavid, who succeeded Kurath as editor of the project in 1964, digested much of the data from the early projects, making many general contributions to Atlas analytical research as well as writing the canonical history of American dialects for Francis' *Structure of American English* (R. McDavid 1958). McDavid's work marked a departure from Kurath's seemingly singular focus on the distribution of linguistic variants with the aim of delineating regional boundaries. McDavid's interest in the intersection of language and culture, as represented by his study of specific words and groups of words, such as *shivaree* (1949, with A. Davis), *hoosier* (1967, with V. McDavid), and *civil war* (1969, also with V. McDavid), added a new dimension to Atlas research, as did his explorations, sometimes with his wife Virginia, of various grammatical phenomena, such as plurals of nouns of *measure* (1964), *ain't* (1941), and so on. Investigations of the intersection of language and social categories continued with data collected by Linguistic Atlas of the Upper Midwest (LAUM) (Allen 1958, 1973–76, 1986a), which, along with LANE, LAMSAS, and the Linguistic Atlas of the North Central States (LANCS), formed the database for several studies by, for instance, the McDavids (1960). R. McDavid wrote one of the first investigations of the differences between black and white speech (1951), while V. McDavid and Allen wrote about sex-related differences in the speech of Atlas informants during this period (e.g., V. McDavid 1956; Allen 1985, 1986b).

The second wave of dialect geography studies was buttressed by advances in technology, including the development of portable audio recorders and the use of computers to store and digest large amounts of linguistic data. Technology laid the groundwork for the consideration of LAP responses as "datasets" as well as for the creation of maps made possible by real computing power. With attention turned to computation and modeling, the second wave of LAP studies saw the application of complexity theory to patterns of variation in language.

The LAP materials were passed to Bill Kretzschmar in 1976 and Lee Pederson oversaw interviews for the LAGS from 1968 to 1983. As the director of LAGS, Lee Pederson oversaw modification to the Atlas interview, creating a structure that encouraged a more conversational exchange between interviewer and interviewee. Referring to the "tape/text" (i.e., the transcribed interviews), Pederson noted that Atlas data is ripe for discourse analysis and narrative analysis, stating that "the text suggests possibilities that extend beyond the primary targets of linguistic geography, the worksheet items. It points toward interdisciplinary research that offers unedited materials to study language as action, structure, art" (1993, p. 38). (As it turns out, Pederson's statement foreshadowed the intersection of the LAP and the third-wave studies to come.) Adjustments to the Atlas interview structure were not the only changes made during this period. Kretzschmar (1996) explains the main difference between the generations of LAP editors as being a shift in focus from mapping isoglosses to investigating the variation within the response databases:

> When Pederson and I read Kurath's analytical works, we usually look at the treatment of individual words, not the summary maps. Pederson's Linguistic Atlas of the Gulf States (1986–92) is monumental because it describes thousands of linguistic features individually, for both regional and social extension. Pederson has made something of a specialty of investigation of topography and land types, such as the Southern Piney Woods or Piedmont regions, and he does map some features together in labeled subareas, but these maps have no isoglosses and do not generate dialect boundaries. It is true to form that Pederson has never attempted an overall description of dialects in the Gulf States. My own work, too, has avoided descriptions of dialects in favor of word studies [. . .]. (Kretzschmar 1996, p. 275)

Though the groundwork for this shift was laid by R. McDavid's earlier work, the second-wave Atlas study changes focus from maps of responses to the responses themselves. The maps that were being made during this period were aimed more at discovery than the delineation of isoglosses and dialect boundaries. For example, Light and Kretzschmar (1996) employ discriminant analysis to create maps that show the "probability of finding a particular linguistic feature at any location in the survey area" (1996, p. 347); see Figure 16 for two examples.

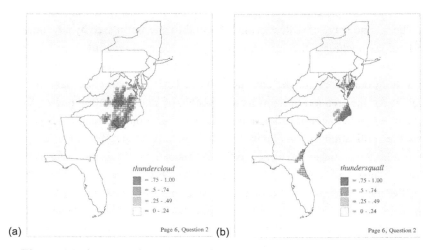

Figure 16 These density maps show the clusters of *thundercloud* (a) and *thundersquall* (b) responses in the mid-Atlantic (Kretzschmar n.p.).

After producing probability maps for hundreds of individual features, Light and Kretzschmar concluded that most feature maps do not produce clear isoglosses, instead finding features whose distributions are not complementary (like those of *pallet* and *bunk* from Section 2.1) as well as large areas of "mixed usage" that go beyond any kind of transition area near identified dialect boundaries (p. 348). Discussions such as those presented in Light and Kretzschmar go beyond simply questioning older ideas about regional dialects, they provide a model for conducting data-driven inquiries of LAP materials.

New computational methods continued to influence the second wave of Linguistic Atlas studies, sparking academic dialogues about the Midland dialect region as a region that should be further divided into North Midland and South Midland (Bailey 1968; Carver 1987), as a "large linear transition area" that should not be considered a separate "dialect" (Davis & Houck 1992, p. 62), or as a "distinct dialect area" whose core is Appalachian English (Johnson 1994, p. 419). None of the statistical analyses, performed on large LAMSAS datasets, would have been possible in earlier times.

In addition, the passage of time made it possible to carry out a real-time study of language change. Johnson (1996) showed creativity and foresight that put her work on the cutting edge (perhaps even still) of Linguistic Atlas studies. Her methodology was an inspired mix of old and new. She interviewed informants from NC, SC, and GA in the early 1990s who were similar in terms of their social characteristics to speakers interviewed in those states in the 1930s. She used a subset of the targets from the earlier survey as well as a similar interview style. But, explicitly lining up the newly collected data with data from the original LAMSAS survey went well beyond the confines of first-wave dialectology, as she was able to talk about both language variation and language change, the latter from a real-time study perspective. Johnson looked for statistical correlations between speakers' membership in various social categories (e.g., age, sex, ethnicity) and the use of approximately 485 individual variants. Her analyses revealed that, for the original LAMSAS data collected in the 1930s, region accounted for the largest percentage of correlations found, while, for the 1990s data, "variation based on region of residence [. . .] declined, while age, sex, and race have become relatively more important" (1996, p. 31). In terms of language change, Johnson found that although there were "fewer regionally-based variants" in 1990 than were identified in the 1930s, "the number of lexical choices available seems to be growing" and notes also that "such growth allows room for tremendous diversification" (1996, p. 92). There might have been fewer variants with localized use present in the 1990s data, but the increase in the total number of variants available to speakers leaves the door open for speakers to use individual variants as a means of creating social meaning and/or personal and community identities (i.e., this kind of change leaves the linguistic door open for enregisterment processes to unfold).

While the geographic and social distributions of responses were still considered important, Kretzschmar (and others) began looking at what the numerical distribution of responses could tell us about the nature of variation and of language itself. The ability to assess Atlas responses in database form as "big data" suggested language is a complex system and that the pattern of variation found in Atlas data – that of the asymptotic hyperbolic curve (a-curve) – is found at all levels of data, across data sets organized by region or state, by sex, or by ethnicity, and for all types of language data: lexical, phonological and grammatical (Kretzschmar 2009, 2015, 2018; Burkette 2011, 2012, 2013). The a-curve shows us the shape of LAP data, as evidenced by the LAMSAS and LAGS datasets presented in Sections 5.2 and 5.3, which can be generalized; LAP datasets (usually) have a small set of core terms that are given as responses by the majority of informants, accompanied by a large set of peripheral terms that are given as responses by only a few speakers (usually only one or two). Figure 17 contains the a-curves for the LAMSAS and LAGS "thunderstorm" data.

As the datasets in Section 5 and the a-curves in Figure 17 show, the LAMSAS and LAGS "thunderstorm" data share the core/periphery distribution. Taking the responses that occurred over 100 times as the core responses,[17] we see that the earlier LAMSAS core (*thunderstorm, thundershower, storm*, and *thundercloud*) is slightly different from the more recent LAGS core (*thunderstorm, electrical storm*, and *storm*). One way to think about LAP data in light of its distribution as an a-curve is to evaluate what happens to terms along the curve: which terms remain core responses over time (*thunderstorm* and *storm*, in this case), which terms used to be core and then fall out of use (e.g., *thundercloud*, which occurred over 100 times in LAMSAS but only seven times in LAGS), and which terms move from the periphery to the top of the curve. Thus, the a-curve gives us an idea of both the scope and shape of variation as well as an idea of how a language dataset changes over time.

The technological and theoretical developments of the second wave in American dialectology made possible these new approaches to LAP data. Additionally, since 2018, there has been a concerted effort to organize and inventory all of the LAP materials, a process that has uncovered (or rediscovered) Atlas data that have never been considered before (or hasn't been considered in a long time). New approaches

---

[17] One hundred (100) occurrences is being used as a benchmark for core terms in this example. The line between "core" terms and "peripheral" ones is not a precise measurement, however; generally speaking, the frequency of responses shows a steep drop-off when moving from core to peripheral.

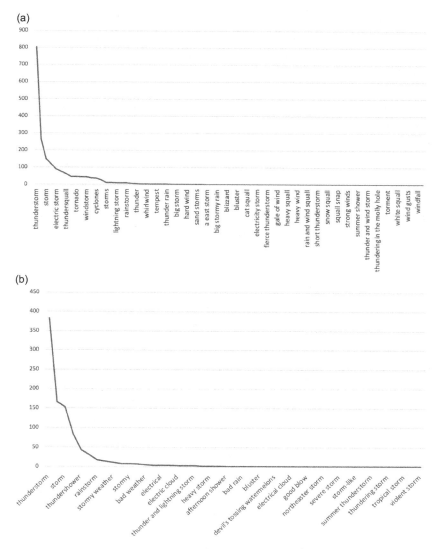

Figure 17 The a-curve for LAMSAS "thunderstorm" (a) and LAGS "thunderstorm" (b).

and "new" data have provided the stage for a new wave in dialect study, which begs the question: What does a third-wave linguistic atlas look like?

6.3 Third-Wave Dialectology

Linguistic geography has changed a great deal since its inception in Europe over a century ago, and the trajectory of large surveys like the LAP needs to continue to change to align with the goals and understandings of contemporary social sciences.

The third wave of dialectology will be heralded by increased access to more (and more kinds of) LAP data. Improvements in audio technology have made heritage LAP recordings useful for sociophonetic analysis. Additional progress in the digitization of interview materials has made available LAP data that can be discussed in terms of language regard and language and identity. Viewing Atlas interviews as situated, meaningful, individual interactions opens up transcribed interviews as sites of identity and meaning-making. Older data can also be fodder for inter- and multidisciplinary research as interest in language and material culture grows. However, the only way to engage with (or create) a third-wave LAP is to *use all the data*.[18]

As LAP researchers continue looking into (and looking through) the data we already have, new methods and foci are also being introduced. In many ways, the main challenge for today's LAP is striking a balance between preserving and using to its fullest what we already have on the one hand and, on the other, collecting new data that is relevant to contemporary sociolinguistics and comparable to older LAP collections.

6.3.1 Access to Heritage Audio

Acoustic analysis of LAGS interview recordings from the 1970s and 80s is already underway following the digitization and transcription of sixty-four LAGS interviews that form the Digital Archive of Southern Speech (DASS) (see Kretzschmar et al. 2013 for details). LAGS interviews were recorded on reel-to-reel tapes that were later transferred to cassette (a move not all that helpful for preserving the sound quality), so the DASS recordings had to first be "treated in Praat with a low-pass Hann band filter [...] to eliminate a high-frequency noise" (Renwick & Olsen 2017, p. 409). Renwick and Olsen (2017) were able to use the older recordings to find evidence of both the Southern Vowel Shift and African American Vowel Shift within the LAGS era recordings, though their analysis also found a good bit of inter- and intra-speaker variation (p. 418). Further work with DASS has explored subregional patterning, specifically with regard to southern speakers' use of canonical "Southern" dialect features such as vowel mergers, diphthongization, and monophthongization, revealing a great deal more phonetic variation than expected (Jones & Renwick 2021), yet still supporting general sociolinguistic findings on the trajectory of vowel change in the area (Stanley et al. 2021).

The LAGS recordings offer a time depth of 40–50 years, but the LAP does have recordings that are even older. Fruehwald (2022) outlined procedures

---

[18] Though not directed toward the LAP specifically, "use all the data" has become somewhat of a mantra within (historical) sociolinguistics (Lauersdorf 2018, 2021), and it's a good one at that.

Audio 1 Unprocessed LANE recording. Audio files available to access at
www.cambridge.org/EISO-Burkette

Audio 2 LANE recording that has been cleaned by J. Fruehwald. Audio files
available to access at www.cambridge.org/EISO-Burkette

undertaken to clean up heritage audio such that the 100-year-old LANE record-ings sound strikingly clear. Section 6.3.1 contains two versions of a single short LANE audio clip: an unprocessed version that is representative of the digitized LANE aluminum disks (Audio 1) and a version that has undergone processing (Audio 2). Processing these recordings entails multiple steps to reduce the amount of background noise so that recordings from the early 1930s can be subject to contemporary sociophonetic analysis. After the recordings are cleaned, Fruehwald hopes to develop best practices for the LANE audio, applying speech-to-text technologies, and, after comparing the results with paper transcripts we already have, use corrected transcriptions to derive a forced alignment using the Montreal Forced Aligner (McAuliffe, Socolof, Mihuc, Wagner & Sonderegger 2017) and then analyze vowel formants using the FAVE suite (Rosenfelder et al. 2015).

6.3.2 All the Data

Increased access to data means that individual targets can be explored as they occur across LAP regional projects (as opposed to focusing on targets/distribu-tions within a single regional project). Burkette and Antieau (2022), for instance, compiled data from all available regional surveys for a single feature, the a-prefix. Although the a-prefix is often a standard feature in descriptions of Southern and Appalachian Englishes (e.g., Wolfram & Christian 1976, Feagin 1979, Montgomery & Hall 2004, Montgomery 2009, McQuaid 2017), it was found in LAP data from across the United States (see Figure 18).

Figure 18 offers copious evidence that the a-prefix is not solely a Southern or Appalachian construction, as one finds the feature in the speech of informants from the Northeast, Midwest, and Pacific Coast. Along the lines of suggestions made in Wolfram (2004, p. 81) and Wolfram and Schilling (2016, p. 4), Burkette and Antieau conclude that the a-prefix should likely be considered a rural phenomenon rather than a Southern one (2022, p. 189). They continue:

> Casting the prefix as a rural phenomenon, rather than as a strictly Southern
> one, opens the door to discussions of the feature as a means of indexing

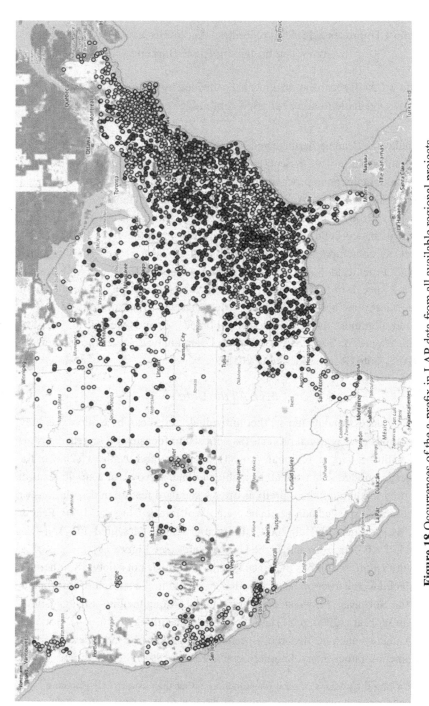

Figure 18 Occurrences of the a-prefix in LAP data from all available regional projects.

participation in (or affinity for) a rural lifestyle, underscoring the potential for the *a-* prefix in identity-making. Additionally, that *a*-prefixing occurs in the most recent LAP interviews suggests that predictions made in the mid-twentieth century of the inevitable demise of the feature may have been a bit premature. (Burkette & Antieau 2022, p. 191)

More work like this needs to be done so that, as a discipline, we have a better understanding of the relationship between large-scale language trends and small-scale language use. A holistic view of LAP data offers a large-scale perspective that smaller, traditional sociolinguistic studies – many of which focus on a single speech community – simply cannot. For this reason, LAP data can contribute to many contemporary sociolinguistics projects, either as a smaller, background component, or as a macro- complement to a micro-oriented investigation.

As the LAP holdings have been unboxed and organized, materials that had been previously tucked away, forgotten about, or otherwise underutilized have been (re)discovered, including data collected via written questionnaires for LAUM (Allen 1972) and LAPC (Reed 1954). For these projects, Reed used data from written questionnaires to fill in geographical gaps where fieldwork had never been done and Allen used questionnaires as support for data collected via face-to-face interviewing. Despite Allen and Reed both recognizing their value, data collected via written questionnaire in the Upper Midwest, the Pacific Coast, and the North Central States have largely lain dormant since their collection, even though a number of contemporary sociolinguists and dialect-ologists have written in support of collecting and using written survey data (e.g., Dollinger 2015; Boberg 2017; Buchstaller et al. 2013; Schleef 2014).

Investigation of the contribution that LAP written questionnaires can make to the study of American English dialects has only just begun (Antieau & Burkette 2023), but preliminary comparisons of interview and survey-collected data from the LAPC have yielded some interesting (and unexpected) findings. Face-to-face interviews were conducted for the LAPC between 1952 and 1959 with 300 residents of California and Nevada. Of those informants, only eleven were non-white and all of them were native speakers of English. Intended as a supplement, questionnaires were also sent out during this time; 1,006 were completed and returned and, of those, 78 respondents were non-white, and a portion of those were non-native English speakers. Figure 19 shows the locations of both sets of LAPC informants. Both the in-person and written aspects of this regional survey show concentrated efforts in California around San Francisco, Los Angeles, and the surrounding urban areas, though the face-to-face coverage of Nevada is a bit better.

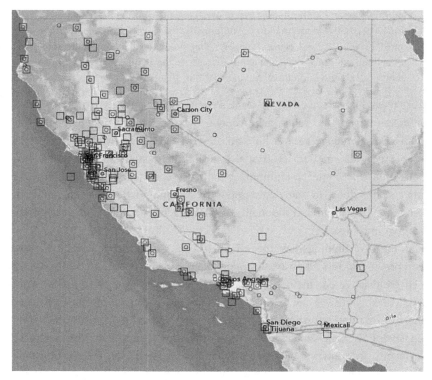

Figure 19 Locations of face-to-face informants (circles) and written
questionnaire informants (squares) from the LAPC.

Figure 20 is an example of the questionnaire's first page, which includes the
directions for completion and the first nine of 100 total questions (the final page
asks respondents for demographic information). Despite the limitations of using
a written survey, such as having answers already provided in a "checklist"
format, the LAPC questionnaire results were not vastly different from responses
garnered by face-to-face interviews in the same region. Not only do the regional
targets chosen from checklists mirror those elicited through in-person interviews, but they also show similar geographic distributions. As an example,
Table 4 contains the top ten in-person interview responses to the "sofa" question
along with all of the responses from the written questionnaires.

The LAPC in-person interviews yielded 880 responses in total, representing 21
response types; the written questionnaires yielded 1.312 responses and 12 response
types. These responses were given at slightly different rates but a general trend (the
high frequency with which *chesterfield* and *davenport* were given, as compared to

For many things in daily life, people in different parts of the United States use different words. As Americans moved westward, they brought with them the terms used in their home states. Studies have already been made of many of the different words used in various areas of the East and Middle West, but a careful study has not been made of word usage in California. On the following pages are a hundred items, which were picked out as examples of these differences. Will you help us in this study by recording your own usage?

DIRECTIONS:

1. Please put a circle around the word in each group which you ordinarily use.

2. IF you ordinarily use more than one word in a group, put a circle around each of the words you use.

3. DON'T put a circle around any word you don't actually use, even though you may be familiar with it.

4. IF the word you ordinarily use is not listed in the group, please write it in the space below the item.

5. IF you never use any word in the group, because you never need to refer to the thing described, don't mark any word.

6. THE MATERIAL IN CAPITALS IS EXPLANATORY ONLY.

EXAMPLE: TOWN OFFICER: selectman,   trustee,   councilman,   commissioner

Thank you,

David W. Reed
Instructor in English
University of California
Berkeley 4, Calif.

1. THE PART OF THE DAY BEFORE SUPPER: afternoon,   evening

2. THE SUN APPEARS AT: dawn,   daybreak,   sunrise,   sun-up

3. THE SUN DISAPPEARS AT: dark,   nightfall,   sun-down,   sunset

4. A TIME OF DAY: a quarter before eleven,   a quarter of eleven,
   a quarter till eleven,   a quarter to eleven

5. RAIN WITH THUNDER AND LIGHTNING: electrical storm,   electric shower,
   electric storm,   shower,   storm,   tempest
   thunder shower,   thunderstorm

6. SUPPORTS FOR LOGS IN FIREPLACE: andirons,   dog irons,   dogs,
   fire irons,   grate,   hand irons,   log irons

7. SHELF OVER FIREPLACE: clock shelf,   fire board,   mantel,
   mantel board,   mantel piece,   shelf

8. WINDOW COVERING ON ROLLERS: blinds,   curtains,   roller shades,

Figure 20 LAPC written questionnaire, first page.

Table 4 LAPC "sofa" responses. (Responses in italics were written in.)

In-person		Written	
Response	Occurrences	Response	Occurrences
Sofa	210	chesterfield	518
chesterfield	149	davenport	276
davenport	149	Sofa	205
Couch	132	Couch	202
Settee	72	Divan	56
Lounge	61	lounge	41
Divan	53	*settee*	6
Daybed	19	*bed*	3
Loveseat	16	*love seat*	3
studio couch	5	*bed divan*	1
(other)	14	*longue*	1

LANE and LAMSAS) is discernable.[19] The questionnaire respondents were slightly more demographically diverse than those interviewed face-to-face, but that seems not to have affected the overall results of the survey. Incorporating written questionnaire responses into the regional survey data, then, seems like a reasonable approach – and one that upholds the "use all the data" mantra.

6.3.3 Expanding What Is Considered "Data"

Recent discoveries have also expanded our ideas about what types of LAP materials can be used as "data." As mentioned in Section 4.1, fieldworkers from the earliest LAP regional surveys produced informant biographies and character sketches, shortened versions of which were reproduced in the LANE and LAMSAS handbooks, Kurath 1939 and Kretzschmar et al. 1994, respectively. Typed and handwritten copies of the original fieldworker-produced documents have been found among the LAP materials, and these are now being analyzed through the lenses of pragmatics and discourse analysis. An example of a typed biographical/character sketch is included here as Figure 21.

These unedited bios and character sketches afford a glimpse into the ideologies and attitudes of the LAP fieldworkers as they evaluated informants' personal and speech characteristics. The sketch in Figure 21, for example,

---

[19] *Chesterfield*, as a term for "sofa," likely came to the US from Canada in the early 1900s, initially entering into American markets in northern California as a term for a particular style of sofa. Eventually, the term came to be used as general term by some US speakers, especially those in the San Francisco area.

```
    247  VA  NEL  EL  K  687
Housewife, 77
Born here
PGF, PGM (of Irish descent) b. here or from down the James
MGF (of Scotch descent), MGM (of English descent), b. here
Attended pay school one session
Methodist
Sweet, simple, sturdy old lady -- very local, but intelligent and
        quick to grasp things in her mountain way
Rather slow tempo with a drawl, causing prolongation of all
        vowels.  FW has not encountered this vowel prolongation east
        of here in Va.  It reminds one of Pa. or N.C.
```

Figure 21 An example of a biographical and character sketch from LANE.

contains the phrase "very local, but intelligent"; the use of *but* here implies that the fieldworker's assumption was that most "locals" would not be "intelligent." Passarelli (2023) explains, "language ideologies in these informant biographies are visible on multiple levels, encoded through both explicit and implicit strategies" noting also that, "fieldworkers align linguistic features and behaviors with social personae and ideological schemas, pointing to processes of enregisterment" (p. 140). Having both the fieldworkers' judgments about their informants and a record of their language use makes it possible to interrogate that language data differently. What linguistic features – vocabulary, pronunciation, grammatical constructions – might have played a role in fieldworker determinations of a speaker's "character"? As Passarelli notes, studies such as McGowan (2011) have demonstrated that "phonetic perceptions are necessarily ideological" (2023, p. 89), which leads to another question: could assumptions made by fieldworkers about speakers' personalities or capabilities, in turn, affect how linguistic features were perceived? These are the kinds of issues that can now be explored within the framework of the LAP.

6.3.4 LAP Interviews as Situated Interactions

An interview is an interaction between a researcher and an informant, and that interaction shapes the structure and outcome of the interview conversation. Penhallurick (2018), in addressing the old idea that the Atlas fieldworker is merely a "word collector" (after Pickford 1956), notes that, like all collectors, the dialectologist is not a passive recipient of their data and that, in the end, "the fate of the dialectologist is to be an active participant in the conversation" (2018, p. 123). The agency of the fieldworker within an LAP interview applies not only to ideological assumptions (as discussed in the previous section), but also to negotiations that take place between the interviewer and interviewee. Understanding these interviews as dynamic and situated interactions means that one can also query LAP data to look at how social meaning is co-constructed during an interview. Full interview transcripts, such as the LAMR examples in Section 5.4, provide an opportunity to examine how people talk about words – how they're used, who uses them, and what they mean. Especially in cases where speakers are aware of multiple terms, pronunciations, or constructions, fieldworkers often ask their subjects about differences between related terms.

For example, thus far, DASS has been used mainly for acoustic analysis (see Section 6.2.1), but Pederson (1993) noted that the collection of full LAGS recordings "offers materials for discourse analysis, (structural) narrative study, and oral literary interpretation" as well as the opportunity "to study language as action, structure, and art" (1993, p. 38). What follows is an excerpt from one of the DASS transcripts with informant GA100 in which we witness the negotiation of word meaning and home spaces.

```
Interviewer: Okay, mm-hmm. Um, and what do you call a piece of
furniture in the bedroom that has drawers in it that you put
clothes in?
GA100: Dresser?
Interviewer: Mm-hmm. Does that have a mirror?
GA100: Yes.
Interviewer: Alright, what about one that doesn't have a mirror?
GA100: A chest of drawer.
Interviewer: Mm-hmm, alright. What would you call a piece of
furniture in a bedroom that might have two doors, and you can hang
clothes in it and maybe drawers at the bottom? It's an old-
fashioned thing.
GA100: Mmm
Interviewer: Ever see that?
GA100: No.
Interviewer: Did you ever hear of a chifforobe or a wardrobe?
GA100: I heard wardrobe, but I ain't heard, I thought you just put
it in the closet.
Interviewer: Okay, uh, so you just lived in houses that had
closets?
GA100: Yeah.
Interviewer: This, these they had in old-fashioned times, is
when they didn't have closets.
```

Clearly, different kinds of homes contain various storage spaces for items of clothing. Some of these are free-standing pieces of furniture, named here as *dresser* and *chest of drawer* by GA100 and *wardrobe* as suggested by the interviewer, while a built-in storage space is generally referred to as a *closet*. This exchange hints at a connection between the kinds of homes an interviewee had lived in and the vocabulary at their disposal. GA100 indicates that they have heard the term *wardrobe*, but don't necessarily know what the term refers to (at least in terms of bedroom furniture). It is the interviewer, then, that creates for the interviewee a connection between *wardrobe* and the characterization of "old-fashioned."

In regard to viewing this is a situated interaction: Does it alter the way you read this exchange to know that GA100 was a high school student? How about knowing that GA100 was a fifteen-year-old African American male high school student from Atlanta and the interviewer was a white woman in her mid-twenties who had a PhD? If any aspect of this demographic information caused even the slightest re-evaluation of the exchange, then there's a discussion to be had about interactional and situated meaning-making.

6.3.5 Third-Wave Mapping

Map-making is, and always has been, a "theory-driven enterprise" (Kretzschmar 2003, p. 130) and linguistic theory has grown up a lot since the days of Hans Kurath and Raven McDavid, which means that the maps we make with LAP data have to grow up too. Traditional dialectology focused on the regional distribution of linguistic variables, and although making maps by hand was tedious, it was conceptually easy enough to plot variables in two dimensions. Today, however, third-wave mapping calls on us to incorporate additional dimensions as we grapple with the concepts of spatiality and movement. Spatiality (a concept parallel to that of "materiality" in archaeology) extends our understanding of space beyond the physical. Spaces are always social; they are created by social interactions and are "always in a state of becoming" (Britain 2010, p. 72). Spaces are dynamic; they are created by social, political, and economic interactions and it is within these inter-actions that we find spatiality. In addition, people move around, individually and idiosyncratically, but also habitually and in groups – what Laura Wright refers to as communities of spatial practice. So how do we represent spaces that are inherently social on a map?

Maps need to account for informants who may be multilingual, mobile, and members of an array of social categories. Pluridimensional cartography includes the simultaneous mapping of geolocation with social and temporal factors (Thun 2010, pp. 507–508). The map in Figure 22 shows the distribution of the lexical item *chest of drawers* across regions and across generations; the oldest speakers are represented

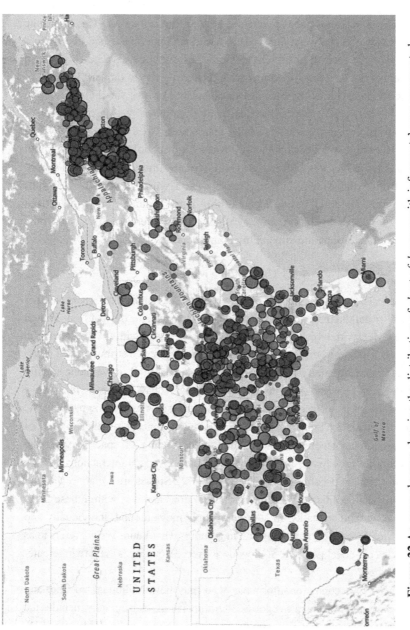

Figure 22 An example map showing the distribution of *chest of drawers* with informants' ages represented by the circle size (the largest circles represent the oldest speakers).

by the largest circles. In this case, we're looking at location and age, but we could also color code points on the map to represent gender, ethnicity, or education level.

6.4 Updating the LAP Interview

The ultimate goal of the earliest surveys was the delineation of dialect boundaries and the timely capture of data from older respondents. The project was interwoven with the creation of maps of individual linguistic features. Over time, however, the goals and structure of the interview have changed. The overarching goal has shifted from an interest in isoglosses and dialect boundaries to a desire to record variation, to look at the correlations between that variation and specific social and regional groups, and to derive social meanings from these findings (Eckert 2018). Starting in the 1970s, LAP fieldworkers implemented an interview structure that encouraged a more conversational exchange. The most recent LAMR interviews, for example, while still containing questions designed to directly elicit specific targets, tended to be even more conversational, moving toward indirect elicitation of verb forms and other grammatical structures. This updated LAP interview style makes the resulting data both compatible with contemporary sociolinguistic interviews as well as directly comparable to the older, target-oriented ones.

Today's LAP team conducts conversational interviews that still seek names for specific foods, animals, weather phenomena, and so on, as well as morphological and syntactic forms, but use open-ended questions designed to elicit natural speech in response. These new LAP interviews also address the contemporary sociolinguistic interest in perceptions and attitudes via the draw-a-map technique from perceptual dialectology (Cramer 2018; Preston 2018, 2019). The resulting hybrid LAP interview format offers the best of all worlds: a set of dialectological targets that will facilitate comparisons across the LAP surveys and through time, the free-flowing conversation prized by traditional sociolinguistics for grammatical and phonological analysis, and a task that will elicit interviewees' language regard factors about language use in the area.

Contemporary Atlas informant selection addresses the long-standing absence of diversity within the LAP speaker pool, an absence which has not only prevented the LAP from joining conversations about the speech of diverse communities, but has also prevented the project from truly investigating the variation that exists within American English. With the exception of Lorenzo Dow Turner's twenty-one Gullah interviews conducted in 1933, African American and other non-white speakers were grossly underrepresented in the earliest LAP surveys. The 1950s interviews from the western US did little to improve the representation of non-white groups. Three of 51 speakers interviewed for the Linguistic Atlas of the Pacific Northwest (LAPNW) identified themselves as Native American or half-Native American, but of the 300 speakers that make up the LAPC, only 12 were African American. Not until the LAGS interviews of the 1970s was there an attempt at a demographically proportional representation of African American speakers, who make up 26 percent of the LAGS respondent pool. Bilingual speakers and speakers of English as a second language make up an even smaller overall percentage of LAP speakers. Aside from two Pennsylvania German-influenced speakers from LAMSAS and two French-influenced speakers in Louisiana, few surveys included speakers who were not monolingual English speakers, the Linguistic Atlas of Hawai'i (LAH) being a notable exception. Present-day LAP work has modernized respondent selection, taking care to ensure a good representation of the significant communities within the regions where new interviews are being conducted. The decision to expand inclusion of African American and add bilingual and/or heritage speakers of Spanish whose first or primary language may be English is based on the modern sociolinguistic concept of the speech community, one that makes such inclusion an academic essential.

6.5 Key Insights

This final section is intended to address the key insights from dialectology and the LAP, insights that will shape future research as the LAP reaches its centennial and beyond. And while there are a number of "take-home lessons" (if you will) from LAP studies, it is the work being done now that I think will define the LAP's contribution to sociolinguistic study. The last nine decades of Linguistic Atlas study have witnessed a shift in the research goals being set as well as the means by which those goals are being accomplished. (To put it simply, there has been a shift in what we're looking for and where we're looking to find it.)

New ideas and insights, however, do not arise in a vacuum. The meticulous and painstaking work of collecting and preserving the data from thousands of LAP speakers is what makes today's work possible. The advent of new technological capabilities – even those as basic as being able to create a high-resolution digital image of handwritten field notes – has offered researchers the opportunity to work with a wide range of data for investigations of language variation and language change. The first two waves of American dialectology have taught us that:

- Dialects have fuzzy boundaries and should be considered social constructs.
- Variation in language is broader and deeper than one might think.

- LAP datasets can be characterized as having a core and a periphery. What we call a "dialect" probably lives in the middle.
- Researchers should use all the data. Even infrequent responses/variants can be interrogated.
- Generally speaking, the LAP has been underutilized in sociolinguistic studies.

These key ideas form the foundation of the third-wave research presently underway. Today's LAP is fueled by increased access to more data than has been considered before. Whether it's looking at the distribution of features considered "Southern" in order to investigate enregisterment or looking for language ideologies in the writings of fieldworkers, the LAP data floodgates have opened. In her explication of third-wave sociolinguistics, Penny Eckert concluded:

> It has become clear that patterns of variation do not simply unfold from the speaker's structural position in a system of production, but are part of the active – stylistic – production of social differentiation. For years, the study of variation was dominated by a definition of style as "different ways of saying the same thing" (Labov 1972b, p. 323). This definition was compatible with linguists' focus on denotational meaning, with a view of variation as marking social address and with a popular view of style as artifice. But style is at its foundation ideological, and the stylistic form of propositions is very much a part of their meaning. The third wave locates ideology in language itself, in the construction of meaning, with potentially important consequences for linguistic theory more generally. (Eckert 2012, p. 98)

Speakers do not use the language features that they do because they belong to a particular group, and they don't talk the way that they do because of where they live or where they grew up. LAP variants are not simply "different ways of saying the same thing" and LAP fieldworkers are not (and have not ever been) "butterfly collecting." Third-wave dialectology needs to (continue to) consider how knowledge about regional and social identities is produced, and how the distribution of linguistic variables reflects the active social differentiation that Eckert refers to. Third-wave dialectology needs to include discussions of language ideology and needs to contribute to discussions (in sociolinguistics and in related fields such as anthropology and archaeology) about the inter-actional construction of meaning. The LAP should join the larger, ongoing conversations about the speech of diverse communities. We should examine the "how" and "why" of the social meaning created by speakers' use of different (and multiple) variants. And, just because the LAP is changing, doesn't mean that the enterprise has lost its interest in lexical variation; new avenues of investigation, such as the links between language and material culture, can lead us to new destinations for talking about vocabulary. These ideas represent both the past and the future; pieces of old ideas are being unhooked from the frameworks that previously constrained them and new ideas are expanding to fill the spaces created by new theories and new questions. As a collective, the LAP welcomes these new initiatives as we actively work to construct a Linguistic Atlas for the twenty-first century.

6.6 Key Readings

Burkette, A. (2001). The Story of Chester Drawers. *American Speech*, *76*(2), 139–157.

Chambers, J., & Trudgill, P. (1980). *Dialectology*. Cambridge: Cambridge University Press.

Johnson, E. (1996). *Language Variation and Change in the Southeastern United States: 1930–1990*. Tuscaloosa: University of Alabama Press.

Kretzschmar, W. A., Jr. (2003). Mapping Southern English. *American Speech*, *78*(2), 130–149.

Kretzschmar, W. A., Jr., McDavid, V. G., Lerud, T. K., & Johnson, E. (Eds.). (1993). *Handbook of the Linguistic Atlas of the Middle and South Atlantic States*. Chicago, IL: University of Chicago Press.

McDavid, R. I. (1958). The Dialects of American English. In N. Francis, ed., *The Structure of American English*. New York: Ronald, pp. 480–543.

Penhallurick, R. (2018). *Studying Dialect*. London: Palgrave.

References

Agha, A. (2003). The Social Life of a Cultural Value. *Language and Communication, 23,* 321–373.

Agha, A. (2005). Voice, Footing, and Enregisterment. *Journal of Linguistic Anthropology, 15*(1), 38–59.

Alexander, H. (1940). Linguistic Geography. *Queen's Quarterly, 47,* 38–47.

Allen, H. B. (1958). Pejorative Terms for Midwest Farmers. *American Speech, 33,* 260–265.

Allen, H. B. (1972). Curds and Checklists in the Upper Midwest. In L. M. Davis, ed., *Studies in Linguistics in Honor of Raven I: McDavid, Jr.* Tuscaloosa, AL: The University of Alabama Press. 3–7.

Allen, H. B. (1973–1976). *Linguistic Atlas of the Upper Midwest,* 3 vols. Minneapolis: University of Minnesota Press.

Allen, H. B. (1985). Sex-Linked Variation in the Responses of Dialect Informants Part III: Grammar. *Journal of English Linguistics, 19*(2), 149–176

Allen, H. B. (1986a). The Primary Dialect Areas of the Upper Midwest. In H. B. Allen & M. D. Linn, eds., *Dialect and Language Variation.* Orlando: Academic Press. 151–161.

Allen, H. B. (1986b). Sex-Linked Variation in the Responses of Dialect Informants Part III: Grammar. *Journal of English Linguistics, 19*(2), 149–176.

Atwood, E. B. (1953). *A Survey of Verb Forms in the Eastern United States.* Ann Arbor: University of Michigan Press.

Bailey, C. -J. N. (1968). Is There a Midland Dialect of American English? ERIC Document 021 240.

Beckett, D. (2003). Sociolinguistic Individuality in a Remnant Dialect Community. *Journal of English Linguistics, 31*(1), 3–33.

Boberg, C. (2017). Surveys: The Use of Written Questionnaires in Sociolinguistics. In C. Mallinson, B. Childs, & G. Van Herk, eds., *Data Collection in Socio linguistics.* 2nd ed. London: Routledge. 131–141.

Britain, D. (2010). Conceptualizations of Geographic Space in Linguistics. In A. Lamelie, R. Kehrein, & S. Rabanus, eds., *Language and Space: An International Handbook of Linguistic Variation, Volume 2: Language Mapping, Part 1.* Berlin: Mouton de Gruyter. 69–97.

Buchstaller, I. (2013). *Quotatives: New Trends and Sociolinguistic Implications.* Malden, MA: Wiley-Blackwell.

Buchstaller, I., & Khattab, G. (2013). Population Samples. In R. Podesva, ed., *Research Methods in Linguistics*, 4–95.

Burkette, A. (2011). Stamped Indian: History, Localism, and Lexical Variation in Terms for American "Cornbread." *American Speech*, *86*(3), 312–339.

Burkette, A. (2012). Parlor Talk: Complexity from a Historical Perspective. *American Speech*, *87*(4), 391–411.

Burkette, A. (2013). "Garden Sass": Variation Crops Up in Unexpected Places. *Southern Journal of Linguistics*, Fall, *37*(2), 1–16.

Burkette, A., & Antieau, L. (2022). A-prefixing in the Linguistic Atlas Project. *American Speech*, *97*(2), 167–196.

Burkette, A., & Antieau, L. (2023). All of the Above: Incorporating Written Survey Data into Linguistic Atlas Project Studies. Paper presented at the American Dialect Society Conference, Denver, Colorado, January 2023.

Carter, P. M. (2013). Poststructuralist Theory and Sociolinguistics: Mapping the Linguistic Turn in Social Theory. *Language and Linguistics Compass*, *7*(11), 580–596.

Carver, C. M. (1987). *American Regional Dialects: A Word Geography*. Ann Arbor: University of Michigan Press.

Chambers, J., & Trudgill, P. (1980). *Dialectology*. Cambridge: Cambridge University Press.

Cramer, J. (2018). Perceptions of Appalachian English in Kentucky. *Journal of Appalachian Studies*, *24*(1), 45–71.

DARE. (1985–2013). *Dictionary of American Regional English*, 6 vols. Edited by F. G. Cassidy, & J. H. Hall. Cambridge, MA: Belknap Press of Harvard University Press.

Davis, L. M., & Houck, C. L. (1992). Is There a Midland Dialect Area? – Again. *American Speech*, *67*(1), 61.

Davis, A. L., & McDavid, R. I. (1949). "Shivaree": An Example of Cultural Diffusion. *American Speech*, *24*(4), 249–255.

Dollinger, S. (2015). *The Written Questionnaire in Social Dialectology*. Amsterdam: John Benjamins.

Eckert, P. (1989). *Jocks and Burnouts: Social Categories and Identity in the High School*. New York: Teachers College Press.

Eckert, P. (2012). Three Waves of Variation Study: The Emergence of Meaning in the Study of Sociolinguistic Variation. *Annual Review of Anthropology*, *41*(1), 87–100.

Eckert, P. (2018). *Meaning in Linguistic Variation: The Third Wave in Sociolinguistics*. Cambridge University Press

Feagin, C. (1979). *Variation and Change in Alabama English: A Sociolinguistic Study of the White Community.* Washington, DC: Georgetown University Press.

Fruehwald, J. (2022). Doing Sociophonetics with Linguistic Atlas Project Data. Paper presented at Methods in Dialectology XVII, Mainz, Germany, August 02, 2022.

Gilliéron, J., & Edmont, E. (1902). *Atlas linguistique de la France.* Paris: Honore Champion.

Hanley, M. L. (1933). Note on the Collection of Phonographic Records. *Dialect Notes (Publications of the American Dialect Society), VI*(Part VII), 368.

Hazen, K. (2015). Forging Third-Wave Dialectology. *Dialectologia, 15*, 69–85.

Jaberg, K., & Jud, J. (1928). *Sprach- und Sachatlas des Italiens und der Südschweiz.* Zofingen: Ringier.

Johnson, E. (1994). Yet Again: The Midland Dialect. *American Speech, 69*(4), 419.

Johnson, E. (1996). *Language Variation and Change in the Southeastern United States: 1930–1990.* Tuscaloosa: University of Alabama Press.

Johnstone, B., Andrus, J., & Danielson, A. (2006). Mobility, Indexicality, and the Enregisterment of "Pittsburghese." *Journal of English Linguistics, 34*, 77–104.

Jones, J. A., & Renwick, M. E. L. (2021). Spatial Analysis of Sub-Regional Variation in Southern US English. *Journal of Linguistic Geography, 9*(2), 86–105.

Kretzschmar, W. A., Jr. (1996). Foundations of American English. In E. Schneider, ed., *Focus on the USA.* Philadelphia, PA: John Benjamins. 25–50.

Kretzschmar, W. A., Jr. (2003). Mapping Southern English. *American Speech, 78*(2), 130–149.

Kretzschmar, W. A., Jr. (2009). *Linguistics of Speech.* Cambridge: Cambridge University Press.

Kretzschmar, W. A., Jr. (2015). *Language and Complex Systems.* Cambridge: Cambridge University Press.

Kretzschmar, W. A., Jr. (2018). *The Emergence and Development of English.* Cambridge: Cambridge University Press.

Kretzschmar, W. A., Jr., Bounds, P., Hettel, J., et al. (2013). The Digital Archive of Southern Speech (DASS). *Southern Journal of Linguistics, 37*(2), 17–38.

Kretzschmar, W. A., Jr., McDavid, V. G., Lerud, T. K., & Johnson, E. (Eds.). (1993). *Handbook of the Linguistic Atlas of the Middle and South Atlantic States.* Chicago, IL: University of Chicago Press.

Kretzschmar, W. A., Jr. , Renwick, M. E. L., Lipani, L. M., et al. (2019). Transcriptions of the Digital Archive of Southern Speech. www.lap.uga .edu/Projects/DASS2019/.

Kurath, H. (1930). Report of Interviews with European Scholars Concerning Our Plans for a Linguistic Atlas of American English. *Dialect Notes (Publications of the American Dialect Society)*, *VI*(Part 2), 73–74.

Kurath, H. (1933). Progress of the Linguistic Atlas. *Dialect Notes (Publications of the American Dialect Society)*, *VI*(Part VII), 365–367.

Kurath, H. (1939). *Handbook of the Linguistic Geography of New England.* Washington, DC: American Council of Learned Societies.

Kurath, H. (1949). *A Word Geography of the Eastern United States.* Ann Arbor: University of Michigan Press.

Kurath, H., Haney, M., Bloch, B., Lowman, G., & Hansen, M. (1972). *Linguistic Atlas of New England*, 3 vols. New York: AMS Press.

Kurath, H., Hansen, M., Bloch, B., & Bloch, J. (1973). *Handbook of the Linguistic Geography of New England.* 2nd ed. New York: AMS Press.

Kurath, H., & McDavid, R. I., Jr. (1961). *The Pronunciation of English in the Atlantic States.* Ann Arbor: University of Michigan Press.

Labov, W. (1966). *The Social Stratification of English in New York City.* Cambridge: Cambridge University Press.

Labov, W. (1972b). *Sociolinguistic Patterns.* Philadelphia: University of Pennsylvania Press.

Lauersdorf, M. R. (2018). Linguistic Visualizations as objets d'art? In N. Bubenhofer, & M. Kupietz, eds., *Visualisierung sprachlicher Daten [Visualization of Linguistic Data].* Heidelberg: Heidelberg University. 91–122.

Lauersdorf, M. R. (2021). Historical Sociolinguistics and the Necessity of Interdisciplinary Collaboration. In A. Burkette, & T. Warhol, eds., *Crossing Borders, Making Connections: Interdisciplinarity in Linguistics.* Berlin: Mouton de Gruyter. 207-230

Lee, J., & Kretzschmar, W. A. (1993). Spatial Analysis of Linguistic Data with GIS Functions. *International Journal of Geographical Information Science*, *7*(6), 541–560.

Light, D., & Kretzschmar, W. A. (1996). Mapping with Numbers. *Journal of English Linguistics*, *24*(4), 343–357.

McAuliffe, M., Socolof, M., Mihuc, S., Wagner, M., & Sonderegger, M. (2017). Montreal Forced Aligner: Trainable Text-Speech Alignment Using Kaldi. *Proc. Interspeech,* 2017, 498–502

McDavid, R. I. (1941). Ain't I and Aren't I. *Language*, *17*(1), 57–59.

McDavid, R. I. (1948). Postvocalic /r/ in South Carolina: A Social Analysis. *American Speech*, *23*(3/4), 194–203.

McDavid, R. I. (1958a). Linguistic Geographic and Toponymic Research. *Names*, *6*(2), 65–73.

McDavid, R. I. (1958). The Dialects of American English. In N. Francis, ed., *The Structure of American English*. New York: Ronald. 480–543.

McDavid, V. G. (1956). Verb Forms of the North Central States and Upper Midwest. Ph.D. diss., University of Minnesota.

McDavid, R. I., Jr. (with V. G. McDavid). (1964). Plurals of Nouns of Measure in the United States. In A. H. Marckwardt, ed., *Studies in Language and Linguistics in Honor of Charles C. Fries*. Ann Arbor: The English Language Institute. 271–301.

McDavid, R. I. (1967). Historical, Regional, and Social Variation. *Journal of English Linguistics*, *1*(1), 25–40.

McDavid, R. I., & McDavid, V. (1951). The Relationship of the Speech of American Negroes to the Speech of Whites. *American Speech*, *26*(1), 3–17.

McDavid, R. I., & McDavid, V. (1960). Grammatical Differences in the North Central States. *American Speech*, *35*(1), 5–19.

McDavid, R. I., Jr. & McDavid, V. (1969). The Late Unpleasantness: Folk Names for the Civil War. *Southern Journal of Communication*, *34*(3), 194–204.

McDavid, R. I., Jr. & McDavid, V. (1973). Cracker and Hoosier. *Names*, *21*(3), 161–167.

McDavid, V. (1986). The Social Distribution of Selected Verb Forms in the Linguistic Atlas of the North Central States. In H. B. Allen & M. D. Linn, eds., *Dialect and Language Variation*. Orlando: Academic Press. 239–246.

McGowan, K. B. (2011). *The Role of Socioindexical Expectation in Speech Perception*. Doctoral dissertation, University of Michigan, Ann Arbor.

McQuaid, G. A. (2017). A Comprehensive Survey of A-prefixing in Southern Appalachia. *Language and Linguistics Compass*, *11*(5), e12242.

Milroy, L. (1987). *Language and Social Networks*. 2nd ed. Oxford: Basil Blackwell.

Montgomery, M. B. (2009). Historical and Comparative Perspectives on A-prefixing in the English of Appalachia. *American Speech*, *84*(1), 5–26.

Montgomery, M. B., & Hall, J. (2004). *Dictionary of Smoky Mountain English*. Knoxville: University of Tennessee Press.

Passarelli, N. A. (2023). "Local, but Intelligent": Language Ideologies in the Informant Biographies of the Linguistic Atlas Project. MA thesis, University of Kentucky.

Pederson, L. (1993). An Approach to Linguistic Geography: The Linguistic Atlas of the Gulf States. In D. Preston, ed., *American Dialect Research*. Amsterdam: John Benjamins. 31–92.

Pederson, L., McDavid, R. I., Foster, C. W., & Billiard, C. E. (Eds.). (1974). *A Manual for Dialect Research in the Southern States*. 2nd ed. Tuscaloosa, AL: University of Alabama Press.

Penhallurick, R. (2018). *Studying Dialect*. London: Palgrave.

Petyt, K. M. (1980). *The Study of Dialect: An Introduction to Dialectology*. Boulder, CO: Westview Press.

Pickford, G. R. (1956). American Linguistic Geography: A Sociological Appraisal. *Word 12*(2), 211–233.

Preston, D. R. (2018). Language Regard: What, Why, How, Whither? In B. Evans, E. Benson, & J. Stanford, eds., *Language Regard: Methods, Variation and Change*. Cambridge: Cambridge University Press. 3–28.

Preston, D. R. (2019). How to Trick Respondents into Revealing Implicit Attitudes – Talk to Them. *Linguistics Vanguard, 5*(s1), art. 20180006.

Reed, D. W. (1954). Eastern Dialect Words in California. *American Speech, 21*, 3–15.

Renwick, M. E. L., & Olsen, R. M. (2017). Analyzing Dialect Variation in Historical Speech Corpora. *Journal of the Acoustical Society of America, 142* (1), 406–421.

Rosenfelder, I., Fruehwald, J., Evanini, K., et al. (2015). FAVE (Forced Alignment and Vowel Extraction) 1.2.2. https://doi.org/10.5281/ zenodo.9846.

Schatzki, T. R. (2001). Practice Minded Orders. In T. Schatzki, K. K. Cetina, & E. von Savigny, eds., *The Practice Turn in Contemporary Theory*. London: Routledge. 42–55.

Schilling-Estes, N. (2004). Constructing Ethnicity in Interaction. *Journal of Sociolinguistics, 8*(2), 163–195.

Schleef, E. (2014). Written Surveys and Questionnaires in Sociolinguistics. In J. Holmes, & K. Hazen, eds., *Research Methods in Sociolinguistics*. Malden, MA: Wiley-Blackwell. 42–57.

Silverstein, M. (2003). Indexical Order and the Dialectics of Sociolinguistic Life. *Language and Communication, 23*, 193–229.

Stanley, J. A., Renwick, M. E. L., Kuiper, K. I., & Olsen, R. M. (2021). Back Vowel Dynamics and Distinctions in Southern American English. *Journal of English Linguistics, 49*(4), 389–418.

Thomas, E. R. (2001). *An Acoustic Analysis of Vowel Variation in New World English*, vol. 85. Durham, NC: Duke University Press.

Thun, Harald. (2010). Pluridimensional Cartography. In A. Lamelie, R. Kehrein, & S. Rabanus, eds., *Language and Space: An International Handbook of Linguistic Variation, Volume 2: Language Mapping, Part 1*. Berlin: Mouton de Gruyter. 506–523.

Trudgill, P. (1972). Sex, Covert Prestige and Linguistic Change in the Urban British English of Norwich. *Language in Society*, *1*(2), 179–195.

Weinreich, U., Labov, W., & Herzog, M. (1968). Empirical Foundations for a Theory of Language Change. In W. Lehmann, & J. Malkiel, eds., *Directions for Historical Linguistics*. Austin, TX: University of Texas Press. 95–188.

Wenker, G. (1888–1923). *Sprachatlas des Deutschen Reichs*. Marburg: Handgezeichnet.

Wolfram, W. (1969). *A Sociolinguistic Description of Detroit Negro Speech*. Washington, DC: Center for Applied Linguistics.

Wolfram, W. (2004). The Grammar of Social and Ethnic Varieties in the Southeast. In B. Kortmann, & E. Schneider, eds., *Handbook of Varieties of English*. Berlin: Mouton de Gruyter. 74–94.

Wolfram, W., & Christian, D. (1976). *Appalachian Speech*. Arlington, VA: Center for Applied Linguistics.

Wolfram, W., & Schilling, N. (2016). *American English: Dialects and Variation*. 3rd ed. Malden, MA: Blackwell.

Acknowledgments

None of this would be possible without the tireless efforts of Lamont Antieau, the Atlas Inventory Specialist and my frequent collaborator, who deserves eternal thanks for his contributions to this and other work produced on the LAP. Thanks also go to my Research Assistant, John Winstead, and to current/recent LAP staff members: Ginny Anderson, Angel Passarelli, Nour Kayali, Catie Mott, and Hunter Huelett. Thanks also to my outstanding colleagues within and outside of my department: Jennifer Cramer, Dennis Preston, Josef Fruehwald, Mark Lauersdorf, Sali Tagliamonte, and Bill Kretzschmar. Though LAP work is often collaborative, I take full responsibility for the information presented here; any errors or omissions should be considered my fault alone.

Cambridge Elements

Sociolinguistics

Rajend Mesthrie

University of Cape Town

Rajend Mesthrie is Emeritus Professor and past head of Linguistics and Research Chair in Linguistics at the University of Cape Town. He was President of the Linguistics Society of Southern Africa (2002–2009) and of the International Congress of Linguists (2013–2018). Among his publications are *The Cambridge Handbook of Sociolinguistics World Englishes* (with R. Bhatt). He was co-editor of *English Today* and editor of the Key Topics in Sociolinguistics series.

Valerie Fridland

University of Nevada, Reno

Valerie Fridland is a Professor of Linguistics at the University of Nevada, Reno. She is the author of *Like, Literally, Dude: Arguing for the Good in Bad English,* and co-author of *Sociophonetics* and lead editor of *Speech in the Western States* series. Her blog, Language in the Wild, appears with *Psychology Today* and her lecture series ‚Language and Society‚ is available through The Great Courses.

About the Series

Sociolinguistics is a vital and rapidly growing subfield of Linguistics that draws on linguistics, sociology, social psychology, anthropology and cultural studies. The topics covered in Cambridge Elements in Sociolinguistics will showcase how language is shaped by societal interactions and in turn how language is a central part of social processes.

Cambridge Elements ≡

Sociolinguistics

Elements in the Series

Conversations with Strangers
William Labov with Gillian Sankoff

Dialectology and the Linguistic Atlas Project
Allison Burkette

A full series listing is available at: www.cambridge.org/EISO

Printed in the United States
by Baker & Taylor Publisher Services